easy one-pot

frugal recipes for busy cooks

RYLAND
PETERS
& SMALL

LONDON NEW YORK

Designer Iona Hoyle
Editors Delphine Lawrance, Helen Ridge
Production Ros Holmes
Art Director Leslie Harrington
Publishing Director Alison Starling

Indexer Hilary Bird

First published in Great Britain in 2009
by Ryland Peters & Small
20–21 Jockey's Fields
London WC1R 4BW
www.rylandpeters.com

10 9 8 7 6 5 4 3 2 1

Text © Nadia Arumguram, Ghillie
Basan, Maxine Clark, Ross Dobson,
Clare Ferguson, Liz Franklin, Tonia
George, Rachael Anne Hill, Louise
Pickford, Jennie Shapter, Sonia
Stevenson, Linda Tubby, Sunil Vijayaker,
Fran Warde, Laura Washburn and
Ryland Peters & Small 2009

Design and photographs
© Ryland Peters & Small 2009

The recipes in this book have been
published previously by Ryland Peters
& Small.

ISBN 978 1 84597 895 2

A CIP record for this book is available
from the British Library.

Printed in China

Notes

• All spoon measurements are level
unless otherwise specified.

• Eggs are medium unless otherwise
specified. Uncooked or partly cooked
eggs should not be served to the
very young, the very old, those with
compromised immune systems or to
pregnant women.

contents

introduction

After a long day at work, the last thing on a lot of people's minds is cooking. It's not merely the thought of having to come up with an idea, but the fact that cooking creates mess and hours of clearing away afterwards. *Easy One-Pot* comes to the rescue of any reluctant cook, providing easy-to-follow recipes that do what they say on the tin; nearly all are cooked in just the one pot, pan or wok, resulting in minimum fuss and little washing up. What is more, the recipes call for easily sourced as well as relatively inexpensive ingredients.

Easy One-Pot is divided into eight sections. Choose from a variety of Soups, salads and light bites, including pasta with melted ricotta and harrira. Omelettes, tortillas and frittatas are ready in no time, with tantalizing combinations such as artichoke and ham tortilla or pepper and chorizo. For a more oriental flavour, the Noodles and stir-fries section covers delights such as pad thai and five-spice duck with aubergine and plums.

Nothing beats a comforting risotto or rice dish on a cold winter's night. Choose from a plethora of dishes in the Risottos and paellas section, with treats such as artichoke and pecorino risotto or lamb pilaf. Mouth-watering Curries and tagines include an aubergine, tomato and lentil curry for vegetarians, and a spicy chicken tagine, bringing a taste of Morocco to the dinner table.

Creamy dishes like potato gratin are included in the Bakes and gratins section, along with hearty options such as baked stuffed pumpkin. Casseroles and stews are the ultimate warming dish to feed a family. More than 25 recipes are included here, from lemony chicken with leeks to Caribbean vegetable stew and from easy fish stew to Vietnamese-style beef. The joy of one pot extends to desserts, with a fig and honey croissant pudding and a white chocolate and raspberry fool among the options.

Easy One-Pot is the perfect solution for low-fuss yet hearty suppers to be shared among family or friends, and will appeal to meat eaters and vegetarians alike.

soups, salads & light bites

The trick with tomato soup is to get a bit of acidity fighting back against the natural sweetness of the tomato. For this, you need sweet tomatoes, but to be sure you can add some brown sugar to compensate – it's up to you to decide how much. The vinegar will then cut through this sweetness.

tomato soup

Put the onions, garlic and oil in a large saucepan, cover and cook over low heat for 10 minutes, stirring occasionally until soft. Do not let it brown.

Add the tomatoes, sugar, vinegar and stock and season well. Bring to the boil, then turn down the heat and simmer for 30 minutes, stirring occasionally.

Transfer to a blender in batches and liquidize until really smooth.

Ladle the soup into bowls and drizzle with chilli oil, if using.

2 red onions, chopped

3 garlic cloves, crushed

4 tablespoons extra virgin olive oil

2 kg plum tomatoes, roughly chopped

1–2 tablespoons soft light brown sugar

2 tablespoons red wine vinegar

750 ml vegetable stock

sea salt and freshly ground black pepper

chilli oil, to serve (optional)

serves 4

This soup is sold all over Morocco. At Ramadan, when most of the country is fasting, there is an eerie silence in the usually bustling souks as stall vendors tuck into their harrira, their first meal after sunset. It can be as rustic as you like, but this version is defined by the subtle flavour of saffron and accompanying spices.

harrira

2 tablespoons extra virgin olive oil

a 475-g lamb shank

2 onions, sliced

3 celery sticks, chopped

3 garlic cloves, chopped

1 teaspoon ground cinnamon

½ teaspoon saffron threads

½ teaspoon ground ginger

several gratings of nutmeg

1 tablespoon tomato purée

4 tomatoes, chopped

700 ml lamb stock or water

200 g tinned chickpeas, drained and rinsed

100 g green lentils, rinsed

freshly squeezed juice of 1 lemon

2 tablespoons freshly chopped coriander

sea salt and freshly ground black pepper

coriander leaves, to garnish

serves 4–6

Heat the oil in a heavy-based casserole, then add the lamb and brown evenly. Add the onions, celery, garlic, cinnamon, saffron, ginger and nutmeg, and season well. Turn the heat down a little, cover and cook for 10 minutes until soft, stirring occasionally.

Stir in the tomato purée and the tomatoes and cook for a further 2–3 minutes. Add the stock, cover and cook for 1 hour until the lamb starts to become tender.

Add the chickpeas and lentils and cook for a further 40 minutes until they are tender and the lamb can easily be pulled off the bone. Shred the meat from the shank, remove the bone and discard. Add lemon juice to taste and check the seasoning (it needs quite a generous amount of salt). Stir in the coriander.

Ladle the soup into bowls and garnish with coriander leaves.

This meal-in-a-bowl soup is loosely based on ribollita, the Tuscan vegetable and bread soup. It's one of those recipes that has three essential elements – good oil, fresh vegetables and good bread. The rest is interchangeable, according to the seasons and your own fancy.

italian vegetable & bread soup

Preheat the oven to 200°C (400°F) Gas 6.

Drizzle the ciabatta slices with a little of the oil and bake in the preheated oven for 5–6 minutes, or until crisp. Remove from the oven and set aside.

Meanwhile, heat 3 tablespoons of the oil in a large saucepan and fry the onions, celery, carrots and garlic over low heat for 4–5 minutes, or until the vegetables are shiny and starting to soften. Add the tomatoes and cook for a further couple of minutes.

Pour in the stock and cook for 15 minutes. Add the cannellini beans and cook for a further 5 minutes. Add the courgettes, kale and savoy cabbage and cook for a further 4–5 minutes, or until the greens are just cooked but still retain their colour.

Break the ciabatta into bite-sized pieces and divide equally between warmed soup bowls. Ladle the soup into the bowls and add a good grinding of pepper. Drizzle with a little more oil and serve immediately.

6 slices of ciabatta bread

about 80 ml extra virgin olive oil

2 red onions, chopped

2 sticks of celery, chopped

2 carrots, chopped

2 garlic cloves, crushed

6 ripe tomatoes, deseeded

1.5 litres vegetable stock

2 x 400-g tins cannellini beans, drained and rinsed

4 courgettes, sliced

200 g kale, chopped

100 g savoy cabbage, shredded

freshly ground black pepper

serves 4

Instead of adding a little fried bacon or pancetta to your minestrone, which is common practice, you can always use Parmesan rind. Buy the cheese in a big chunk and hang on to the rinds in an airtight container in the fridge. Use them for soups like this that need a strong undercurrent; they will add a similar depth of flavour and saltiness.

minestrone soup

4 tablespoons extra virgin olive oil, plus extra to serve

2 carrots, chopped

1 red onion, chopped

4 celery sticks, diced and leaves reserved

6 garlic cloves, sliced

2 tablespoons freshly chopped flat leaf parsley

2 teaspoons tomato purée

400-g tin chopped tomatoes

1 litre hot chicken stock or vegetable stock

400-g tin borlotti beans, drained and rinsed

Parmesan rind (optional)

150 g cavolo nero or spring greens, shredded

100 g spaghetti, broken up

sea salt and freshly ground black pepper

freshly grated Parmesan, to serve

serves 4–6

Heat the oil in a large, heavy-based saucepan, then add the carrots, onion, celery and garlic. Cover and sweat very slowly over low heat, stirring occasionally, until thoroughly softened.

Add the parsley, tomato purée and tinned tomatoes and cook for 5 minutes. Pour in the hot stock and borlotti beans and bring to the boil. If using a Parmesan rind, add this now. Once boiling, add the cavolo nero and simmer for 20 minutes.

Add the spaghetti and cook for 2–3 minutes less than the manufacturer's instructions (by the time you have ladled it into bowls it will be perfectly cooked). Taste and add seasoning if it needs it.

Ladle the soup into bowls and drizzle with extra oil. Serve with a bowl of grated Parmesan to sprinkle over the top.

This is Lebanese in origin, but soups like this are served all over the Middle East. Crispy fried onions are a lovely topping, but you have to be brave and really brown them so they look almost black. In order to do this without burning them, you have to really soften them to start with.

lentil, spinach & cumin soup

Heat the oil in a large, heavy-based saucepan and add the onions. Cook, covered, for 8–10 minutes until softened. Remove half the onion and set aside.

Continue to cook the onion left in the pan for a further 10 minutes until deep brown, sweet and caramelized. Take out and set aside for the garnish.

Return the softened onion to the pan and add the garlic, coriander, cumin seeds and lentils and stir for 1–2 minutes until well coated in oil. Add the stock, bring to the boil, then turn down to a gentle simmer for 30 minutes until the lentils are lovely and soft.

Add the spinach and stir until wilted. Transfer half the soup to a blender and liquidize until you have a purée. Stir back into the soup. Season with lemon juice, salt and pepper.

Ladle the soup into bowls, add a dollop of Greek yoghurt and scatter the pine nuts and fried onions over the top.

3 tablespoons extra virgin olive oil

2 onions, sliced

4 garlic cloves, sliced

1 teaspoon ground coriander

1 teaspoon cumin seeds

150 g brown or green lentils

1.2 litres vegetable stock

200 g spinach

freshly squeezed juice of 1 lemon

sea salt and freshly ground black pepper

4 tablespoons Greek yoghurt, to serve

25 g pine nuts, lightly toasted, to serve

serves 4

Buy only the freshest and best-quality fish for this classic Mediterranean dish. Ask the fishmonger to clean, scale and fillet the fish, and do make sure that he removes all the scales. Good bouillabaisse also features other seafood such as prawns, mussels and clams. If you're feeling rich, you could always add a lobster.

bouillabaisse

100 ml olive oil

1 large onion, diced

2 leeks, thinly sliced

2 garlic cloves, crushed and chopped

1 small bulb of fennel, diced

750 ml passata (sieved tomatoes)

900 ml fish stock

a sprig of thyme

1 fresh bay leaf

a pinch of saffron threads

2 kg fish and shellfish, cleaned, scaled and filleted

sea salt and freshly ground black pepper

warm crusty bread, to serve

serves 4

Heat the oil in a large frying pan. Add the onion, leeks, garlic and fennel and fry the vegetables gently for 5 minutes without letting them brown.

Add the passata, fish stock, thyme, bay leaf, saffron, salt and pepper. Bring to the boil, reduce the heat and simmer for 10 minutes.

Add the pieces of fish and shellfish and cook for 4 minutes.

Carefully lift out the fish fillets and shellfish and divide between 4 large bowls. Ladle over the rich tomato liquid and serve with warm crusty bread.

One of those reliable recipes that just gets better as it matures, ratatouille can be served with many dishes, and also by itself with lots of crusty bread. Don't use green peppers – they are too bitter. Traditionally, aubergines were salted to reduce their bitterness, but if you're really pushed for time, don't bother – today, most types rarely need salting.

ratatouille

Cut the aubergines into large, bite-sized pieces, put them in a colander, sprinkle well with salt and leave to drain for 1 hour. Cut the peppers in half, remove the white membrane and seeds, and slice the flesh into thick strips.

Heat the oil in a heatproof casserole and fry the onions, garlic and coriander seeds until soft and transparent, but not coloured. Add the wine and boil to reduce.

Meanwhile, rinse and drain the aubergines and dry on kitchen paper. Add the peppers and aubergines to the casserole and cook for about 10 minutes, stirring occasionally until softening around the edges, but not browning. Add the tomatoes, sugar and olives. Heat to simmering point, season well with salt and pepper, then half-cover and cook for about 25 minutes. Serve hot or cold. Garnish with basil, if using.

2 aubergines

3 peppers (red, yellow or orange)

3 tablespoons olive oil

2 large onions, thinly sliced

2 garlic cloves, crushed

2 teaspoons finely crushed coriander seeds

5 tablespoons white wine

400-g tin chopped tomatoes

1 teaspoon sugar

about 20 Greek-style dry-cured black olives

sea salt and freshly ground black pepper

basil leaves, to garnish (optional)

serves 6

Mushroom fans will love this tasty mix of juicy mushrooms in a sweet and sour chilli-spiked marinade. It makes a perfect side dish for barbecues. Add a crumbling of salty cheese and you have a pretty special main course for vegetarians too.

marinated mushrooms

60 ml extra virgin olive oil

2 shallots, finely chopped

2 garlic cloves, crushed

500 g brown mushrooms, halved

20 ml apple cider vinegar

2 tablespoons raisins

2 tablespoons runny honey

a pinch of dried chilli flakes

fresh oregano leaves,
to garnish (optional)

serves 4–6

Heat 3 tablespoons of the oil in a frying pan and fry the shallots and garlic over low heat for 2–3 minutes, until softened. Add the mushrooms and fry gently for 4–5 minutes, until golden. Add the cider vinegar and raisins, and bubble for a minute or so. Stir in the honey, remaining olive oil and chilli flakes. Cook for another minute. Remove from the heat and leave to cool. Leave to marinate for half an hour before serving. Garnish with oregano, if using.

Polenta makes a lovely crumb coating on these fish cakes. If using tinned tuna, buy a good-quality brand that has a dense texture and large chunks. Alternatively, pan-cook fresh tuna and flake it yourself.

tuna fish cakes

Cook the sweet potatoes in a pan of simmering water for 20 minutes. Drain well and mash. Add the tuna, spring onions and egg, season and mix well. Divide the mixture into 8 equal pieces and shape into patties.

Put the polenta on a plate and dip the fish cakes in it until coated on all sides.

Heat the oil and fry the fish cakes on each side until golden. Serve with lemon wedges and a tomato salad.

600 g sweet potatoes, peeled and chopped

300 g tuna, flaked

2 spring onions, chopped

1 egg

100 g polenta

3 tablespoons olive oil

sea salt and freshly ground black pepper

1 lemon, cut into wedges, to serve

tomato salad, to serve

serves 4

Pasta is the archetypal fast food. This dish is quick to make and fresh, with the ricotta melting into the hot pasta and coating it like a creamy sauce. The pine nuts give it crunch, while the herbs lend a fresh, scented flavour. If you don't have all the herbs listed here, use just rocket plus one other – the parsley or basil suggested, or perhaps snippped chives.

pasta with melted ricotta

350 g dried penne or other pasta

6 tablespoons extra virgin olive oil

100 g toasted pine nuts

125 g rocket leaves, chopped

2 tablespoons freshly chopped parsley

2 tablespoons freshly chopped basil

250 g ricotta cheese, mashed

50 g freshly grated Parmesan cheese

sea salt and freshly ground black pepper

serves 4

Cook the pasta according to the instructions on the packet. Drain, reserving 4 tablespoons of the cooking liquid, and return both to the pan.

Add the pine nuts and their oil, the herbs, ricotta, half the Parmesan, plenty of black pepper and salt to taste. Stir until the pasta is evenly coated with the sauce.

Serve in warmed bowls, with the remaining cheese sprinkled on top.

For those nights when you want supper in a hurry, this savoury dish can be on the table in just 10 minutes. Serve with basmati and wild rice or couscous, together with some green beans or cabbage.

mustardy mushroom stroganoff

Cook the onion in a covered saucepan with 3 tablespoons of the stock for about 4 minutes or until softened and the liquid has evaporated.

Stir in the mushrooms, garlic and seasoning, then add the remaining stock, mustard and tomato purée. Cook, covered, for 2 minutes, then remove the lid and cook rapidly for 2 minutes to reduce the liquid to a syrup.

Remove from the heat. Stir in the crème fraîche and parsley. Serve immediately on a bed of rice or couscous with green beans or cabbage.

½ small onion, sliced

150 ml vegetable stock

150 g mixed mushrooms, chopped if large

1 garlic clove, crushed

1 teaspoon wholegrain mustard

½ teaspoon tomato purée

1 tablespoon crème fraîche

sea salt and freshly ground black pepper

freshly chopped parsley, to serve

serves 1

No dressing is needed for this dish as the roasting chorizo produces such a wonderful paprika-scented oil. The juices should be really hot so that they wilt the spinach slightly. The combination of sweet potato, meaty chorizo and salty cheese makes this much more than a salad.

sweet potato salad

600 g sweet potatoes, peeled and cut into wedges

2 tablespoons extra virgin olive oil

2 fresh rosemary sprigs, broken up into smaller sprigs

½ teaspoon dried chilli flakes

225 g chorizo, sliced

3 tablespoons sherry vinegar

200 g baby spinach

50 g black olives, stoned and chopped

200 g feta cheese, cut into large chunks

serves 4

Preheat the oven to 190°C (375°F) Gas 5.

Place the sweet potatoes in a roasting tin, drizzle with the oil and sprinkle with the rosemary and chilli flakes. Roast for 10 minutes until beginning to soften.

Add the chorizo and roast for a further 15 minutes until the chorizo is crispy and the sweet potato is softening and charring nicely.

At the end of the cooking time, drizzle over the vinegar and return to the oven for a further 5 minutes.

Put the spinach in bowls and top with the sweet potato, chorizo, olives and feta. Drizzle the juices from the roasting tin over the salad and stir well before serving.

Many Thai salads, soups and stews are flooded with the pungent flavours of Thai basil, mint and coriander. This type of basil is readily available from most Asian shops, but you could use ordinary basil instead.

thai-style beef salad

Put the peppercorns, ground coriander and salt onto a plate and mix. Rub the beef all over with the oil and then put onto the plate and turn to coat with the spices.

Cook the beef in a stove-top grill pan or frying pan for about 10 minutes, turning to brown evenly. Remove from the heat and leave to cool.

Meanwhile, to make the dressing, put the sugar into a saucepan, add the fish sauce and 2 tablespoons water and heat until the sugar dissolves. Leave to cool, then stir in the lime juice, chillies and garlic.

Cut the beef into thin slices and put into a large bowl. Add the cucumber, spring onions, pak-choi and herbs. Pour over the dressing, toss well, then serve.

1 tablespoon black peppercorns, lightly crushed

1 teaspoon ground coriander

1 teaspoon sea salt

500 g whole beef fillet

1 tablespoon groundnut or vegetable oil

1 cucumber, thinly sliced

4 spring onions, thinly sliced

2 baby pak-choi, thinly sliced

a handful of freshly chopped Thai basil

a handful of freshly chopped mint

a handful of freshly chopped coriander

lime dressing

15 g palm sugar or brown sugar

1 tablespoon Thai fish sauce

2 tablespoons lime juice

2 red chillies, deseeded and chopped

1 garlic clove, crushed

serves 4

This is a wonderfully colourful dish, with yellow from the saffron, red from the tomatoes and green from the basil. The potatoes absorb the glorious golden colour and subtle flavour of the saffron as they simmer gently with the tomatoes. Serve warm, as the heat will release the heady aromas of the basil and saffron.

saffron potato salad

500 g large waxy yellow-fleshed potatoes, peeled

a pinch of saffron threads, about 20

8 sun-dried tomatoes (the dry kind, not in oil)

caper & basil dressing

6 tablespoons extra virgin olive oil

3 tablespoons freshly chopped basil leaves, plus extra to serve

2 tablespoons salted capers, rinsed and chopped, if large

1–2 tablespoons freshly squeezed lemon juice, to taste

sea salt and freshly ground black pepper

serves 4

Cut the potatoes into large chunks. Put in a saucepan, add enough cold water to just cover them, then add the saffron and sun-dried tomatoes. Bring slowly to the boil, then turn down the heat, cover and simmer very gently for about 12 minutes until just tender. If the water boils too fast, the potatoes will start to disintegrate. Drain well.

Pick out the now plumped-up sun-dried tomatoes and slice them thinly. Tip the potatoes into a large bowl and add the sliced tomatoes.

To make the dressing, put the oil, chopped basil and capers in a small bowl. Add lemon juice, salt and pepper to taste and mix well. Pour over the hot potatoes, mix gently, then serve hot or warm, scattered with extra basil leaves.

In Italy, this dish is traditionally made with white cannellini beans, but green flageolet beans make an attractive alternative. Fresh tuna can be expensive, so this is a good way of making one wonderful steak stretch a little further.

italian tuna & beans

If using fresh tuna, brush with olive oil and put in a preheated stove-top grill pan. Cook for 3 minutes on each side or until barred with brown but pink in the middle (the cooking time will depend on the thickness of the fish). Remove from the pan, cool and cut into chunks.

Put the oil, onions, garlic and vinegar in a bowl and beat with a fork. Add the beans and toss until well coated.

Add the tuna and basil, salt and pepper. Serve with crusty bread.

1 large tuna steak, about 250 g, or 2 small tins good-quality tuna, about 160 g each, drained

6 tablespoons olive oil, plus extra for brushing

2 red onions, finely sliced

2–3 large garlic cloves, crushed

1 tablespoon sherry vinegar or white wine vinegar

3 x 400-g tins green flageolet beans or white cannellini beans, drained and rinsed, or a mixture of both

4 handfuls of fresh basil leaves and small sprigs

sea salt and freshly ground black pepper

crusty bread, to serve

serves 4–6

Strictly speaking, this isn't a recipe for the traditional Chinese dish but a variation, using a ready-roasted chicken, but you could substitute smoked chicken breasts or even ready-cooked duck from a favourite Chinese restaurant.

bang-bang chicken

a 2.5-kg ready-roasted chicken

3 carrots, peeled and shredded

1 small cabbage, shredded

3 mixed peppers, cut into strips

100 g sugar snap peas, diagonally halved

3 tablespoons toasted sesame oil

50 g sesame seeds

sauce

200 g peanut butter

3–4 tablespoons chilli sauce

2 cm fresh ginger, peeled and grated

3 tablespoons toasted sesame oil

2 tablespoons extra virgin olive oil

serves 4

Put the chicken on a chopping board. Using a rolling pin, give the chicken a few good thwacks along the breast. This will make it much easier to shred. Shred the meat into a large bowl.

Mix together the carrots, cabbage, peppers and sugar snap peas in four individual bowls. Top with the shredded chicken.

Heat the sesame oil in a small frying pan and fry the sesame seeds until golden.

To make the sauce, put the peanut butter, chilli sauce, ginger, sesame oil and olive oil in a saucepan, whisk to combine and heat gently over low heat.

Drizzle some of the sauce over the chicken and scatter with the sesame seeds. Serve immediately, with the remaining sauce alongside.

The creamy horseradish dressing in this recipe is a fabulous complement to the richness of the smoked mackerel, while raw vegetables add crunch and colour. If you wish, you can use couscous instead of bulghur wheat.

mackerel & bulghur wheat salad

Cook the bulghur wheat in a saucepan of lightly salted boiling water for 15 minutes or until tender. Drain, then mix with the lemon juice, chives, yellow pepper and radishes.

Put the spinach leaves into shallow salad bowls, spoon the bulghur wheat on top, then add the flaked smoked mackerel. Mix the dressing ingredients together and drizzle over the fish. Finish with a grinding of black pepper to serve.

60 g bulghur wheat

1 tablespoon freshly squeezed lemon juice

1 tablespoon finely snipped fresh chives

½ yellow pepper, deseeded and diced

8 radishes, sliced

75 g spinach leaves

150 g smoked mackerel fillets, flaked

dressing

3 tablespoons fromage frais

2 teaspoons horseradish sauce

1 teaspoon finely snipped fresh chives

freshly ground black pepper, to serve

serves 2

Dried fenugreek leaves, known as methi in Asian food shops, are not as easy to find as the seeds, but they have a unique flavour that scents the dish and makes it something out of the ordinary. If you can't find methi, use dried mint instead, or omit altogether. Use enough chillies to suit your taste.

spicy chickpeas

1 tablespoon groundnut or mustard oil

2 teaspoons ground turmeric

2 teaspoons black mustard seeds

2 onions, chopped

2 garlic cloves, chopped

1 tablespoon dried fenugreek leaves (optional)

4 tomatoes, skinned, halved and deseeded

3–5 fresh red chillies, halved, deseeded if preferred, then chopped

2 x 400-g tinned chickpeas, drained and rinsed

sea salt, to taste

fresh fenugreek leaves, to serve (optional) *

serves 4

Heat the oil in a casserole, add the turmeric and mustard seeds and heat until the seeds pop. Add the onions and garlic and fry gently until softened and lightly browned. Add the dried fenugreek leaves, if using, tomatoes and chillies. Cook at a low heat until the tomatoes have melted down to form a sauce.

Add the chickpeas to the casserole. Turn to coat with the mixture and cook until hot. Add salt to taste. Serve, topped with sprigs of fresh fenugreek leaves, if using.

* Fresh fenugreek leaves are sold in Indian greengrocers. They are cooked and served like spinach, but a few sprigs make a delicious garnish. Omit if they are hard to find.

omelettes, tortillas & frittatas

A whole breakfast made without fuss in one pan, just like a giant omelette – a British version of Italian frittata. Use the best bacon you can find and fresh, free-range eggs.

bacon & eggs in a pan

Set a large, non-stick frying pan over medium heat. Add the oil, heat, then add the bacon. Cook for 2 minutes until the bacon starts to brown and go crisp around the edges.

Break the eggs into a bowl, add salt and pepper and whisk lightly. Pour into the pan around the bacon, making sure the base is covered and the bacon sits half-submerged. Dot with the tomatoes and cook over medium to low heat until the eggs have set. Sprinkle with chives and serve immediately, cut into wedges.

1 tablespoon sunflower oil

8 slices dry-cured back bacon

6 large eggs

10 cherry tomatoes, halved

2 tablespoons finely snipped fresh chives

sea salt and freshly ground black pepper

serves 4

This omelette is fast to make, nice to look at and easy to eat. Add some sliced sausages if you like, and serve hot or cold, with a mixed leaf salad and crusty bread or pita.

greek-style omelette

100 g cherry tomatoes, halved

4–5 bottled golden hot peppers, drained and sliced

3 spring onions, sliced

40 g pitted black olives, sliced

100 g feta cheese

a small handful of freshly chopped flat leaf parsley

6 large eggs

sea salt and freshly ground black pepper

olive oil, for frying

salad

200 g mixed leaves

1 tablespoon freshly squeezed lemon juice (a little less than ½ lemon)

4 tablespoons extra virgin olive oil

sea salt and freshly ground black pepper

serves 2–4

Preheat the oven to 200°C (400°F) Gas 6.

Rub a deep frying pan with olive oil, then arrange the tomatoes, hot peppers, spring onions and olives equally around it. Crumble in the feta, then grind pepper over the top. Sprinkle with parsley.

Put the eggs in a bowl, beat well and season with a good pinch of salt. Pour over the ingredients in the pan. Bake in the preheated oven until puffed and just golden around the edges, 15–20 minutes.

To make the salad, put the leaves in a bowl, add the lemon juice, oil, salt and pepper. Toss well, taste and adjust the seasoning with more salt and pepper if necessary. Serve with the omelette cut into wedges – hot, warm or at room temperature.

Traditionally, a Spanish tortilla is made with potatoes and onions, but this quicker variation uses peppers and chorizo. You could, though, use just onions, any kind of cheese, tomatoes, courgettes, ham or salami. Experiment! This is good for breakfast, brunch, lunch, dinner or a late-night snack, and can be served hot or cold.

pepper & chorizo tortilla

Heat the oil in a large, non-stick frying pan. Add the peppers and onion and cook over medium-high heat until golden brown, 3–5 minutes. Add the garlic and chorizo, cook for 2–3 minutes. Season with a pinch of salt and set aside.

Whisk the eggs in a bowl. Stir in the parsley, season with ¼ teaspoon salt and pepper to taste, then pour over the peppers in the pan. Sprinkle with the cheese.

Cover and cook over low heat until set around the edges but still barely wobbly in the middle, 10–12 minutes. Loosen the sides and underneath with a plastic spatula. You should be able to slide the tortilla out of the pan and onto a plate, then flip onto another plate to serve bottom-side up. If it cannot be shaken out of the pan, put a large plate upside down over the frying pan, hold the edges with oven gloves and flip over to release the tortilla. Serve hot, warm or cold.

2 tablespoons extra virgin olive oil

1 red pepper, thinly sliced

1 yellow pepper, thinly sliced

1 onion, thinly sliced

2 garlic cloves, chopped

125 g chorizo, sliced

6 large eggs

a handful of freshly chopped flat leaf parsley

40 g freshly grated Manchego cheese

sea salt and freshly ground black pepper

serves 4–6

The traditional tortilla must be one of the world's most accommodating dishes. It's good for almost any occasion – picnic food, a quick lunch dish eaten between slices of bread, even a breakfast snack – and this variation, which includes garlic, is no exception. Served with a scarlet piquillo sauce, it is delicious.

spanish potato omelette

2 tablespoons extra virgin olive oil

1 kg salad potatoes, peeled and cut into 2-cm cubes

1 onion, sliced into rings

4 garlic cloves, finely chopped (optional)

6 eggs, beaten

4 tablespoons freshly chopped flat leaf parsley or spring onion tops

sea salt and freshly ground black pepper

piquillo sauce

225-g jar or tin of roasted piquillo peppers or pimientos

3 tablespoons sherry vinegar

serves 4–6

Heat the oil in a medium frying pan, add the potatoes and onion and cook over low heat for 12–14 minutes or until tender but not browned, moving them about with a fish slice so that they cook evenly. Add the garlic, if using, for the last 2 minutes.

Put the eggs in a bowl, season with salt and pepper and beat well.

Using a slotted spoon, remove the cooked potatoes, onion and garlic from the pan and stir them into the egg mixture. Stir in the parsley.

Quickly pour the mixture back into the hot frying pan. Cook, not stirring, over low to moderate heat for 4–5 minutes or until firm, but do not let it brown too much. The top will still be wobbly, only part-cooked.

Holding a plate over the top of the omelette, quickly invert the pan, omelette and plate. Slide the hot omelette back, upside down, to brown the other side for 2–3 minutes more, then remove from the pan and leave to cool for 5 minutes.

To make the sauce, put the piquillo peppers, 6 tablespoons of the liquid from the jar (make it up with water if necessary) and the sherry vinegar in a blender. Purée to form a smooth, scarlet sauce.

Cut the omelette into chunks, segments or cubes. Serve the sauce separately, spooning some over the pieces of tortilla.

Ideal for a lunch or supper dish, or perfect for al fresco dining served with a crisp salad, this omelette is just bursting with flavour. It is worth buying tomatoes ripened on the vine for their extra taste explosion.

feta cheese & tomato open omelette

Break the eggs into a bowl and whisk briefly with a fork, just enough to mix the yolks and whites. Season with salt and pepper, add 2 tablespoons water and the basil, mint and spring onions then mix briefly.

Heat the oil in a large non-stick frying pan. Pour in the egg mixture and cook over medium heat for 4–5 minutes, drawing the mixture from the sides to the centre until the omelette is half cooked.

Top with the feta and the tomato halves, cut side up, and cook for 2 minutes. Slide under a preheated grill and cook until light golden brown. Slide onto a warmed plate and serve immediately.

5 large eggs

2 tablespoons freshly chopped basil

1 tablespoon freshly chopped mint

3 spring onions, finely chopped

2 tablespoons sunflower oil

75 g feta cheese, crumbled

8 small cherry tomatoes, halved

sea salt and freshly ground black pepper

serves 2

This frittata has a real Mediterranean feel and is flavoured with some of Italy's favourite ingredients – olives, sun-dried tomatoes and Parmesan cheese. If you have the time, it is worth mixing the tomatoes and sage into the eggs up to an hour before cooking for a more intense flavour.

sun-dried tomato frittata

6 large eggs

8 sun-dried tomatoes in oil, drained and sliced

1 tablespoon freshly chopped sage

50 g pitted black olives, thickly sliced

50 g freshly grated Parmesan cheese, plus extra shavings to serve (optional)

2 tablespoons extra virgin olive oil

1 onion, halved and sliced

sea salt and freshly ground black pepper

serves 2–3

Break the eggs into a large bowl and whisk briefly with a fork. Add the sun-dried tomatoes, sage, olives, Parmesan, salt and pepper and mix gently.

Heat the oil in a large non-stick frying pan, add the onion and cook over low heat until soft and golden.

Increase the heat to moderate, pour the egg mixture into the pan and stir just long enough to mix in the onion. Cook over medium-low heat until the base of the frittata is golden and the top has almost set.

Slide the pan under a preheated grill to finish cooking or put a plate on top of the pan and invert the pan so the frittata drops onto the plate. Return the frittata to the pan, cooked side up, and cook on top of the stove for 1–2 minutes.

Transfer to a serving plate, top with Parmesan shavings, if using, and serve hot or cold, cut into wedges.

Porcini are difficult to buy fresh, but are widely available dried. They are one of the best mushrooms, with an intense, rich flavour that will pervade the omelette. Strain the soaking liquid from the porcini and add a spoonful to the omelette mixture, or keep it for a soup or stew.

porcini frittata

Put the porcini in a small bowl and cover with warm water. Leave to soak for 30 minutes. Break 1 of the eggs into a bowl, add the mascarpone and mix well. Add the remaining eggs and whisk briefly with a fork. Stir in the parsley and season with salt and pepper.

Heat 1 tablespoon of the oil in a large non-stick frying pan, add the onion and cook over low heat until soft. Add another tablespoon of oil and the button mushrooms and cook for 5 minutes. Drain the porcini and chop if large. Add to the pan and cook for 2 minutes.

Using a slotted spoon, transfer the mushrooms and onions into the egg mixture and stir gently.

Wipe out the frying pan with kitchen paper, add the remaining oil and heat gently. Add the frittata mixture and cook over low heat until browned on the underside and nearly set on top. Sprinkle with Parmesan and slide under a preheated grill to finish cooking the top and melt the cheese. Transfer to a warm serving plate.

Melt the butter in the frying pan, add the wild mushrooms and fry quickly. Spoon over the top of the frittata and serve.

15 g dried porcini mushrooms

6 eggs

50 g mascarpone cheese

3 tablespoons freshly chopped flat leaf parsley

3 tablespoons extra virgin olive or sunflower oil

1 onion, halved and sliced

125 g button mushrooms, sliced

1 tablespoon freshly grated Parmesan cheese

15 g unsalted butter

75 g fresh wild mushrooms

sea salt and freshly ground black pepper

serves 2–3

A speciality of the Alicante region of Valencia is an unusual meat paella finished with an omelette topping. For this mouth-watering tortilla, the meat has been replaced with shellfish typical of Paella Valenciana.

paella tortilla

3 tablespoons extra virgin olive or sunflower oil

1 skinless chicken breast, about 175 g, cut into strips

1 medium onion, chopped

1 garlic clove, chopped

1 red pepper, halved, deseeded and sliced

2 tomatoes, chopped

100 g paella rice

a pinch of saffron threads, soaked in 2 tablespoons hot water

250 ml chicken stock

150 g ready-mixed seafood, such as prawns, mussels and squid rings *

6 eggs

3 tablespoons frozen peas, thawed

sea salt and freshly ground black pepper

serves 4–6

Heat 2 tablespoons of the oil in a large non-stick frying pan, add the chicken and fry until browned. Transfer to a plate.

Add the onion, garlic and red pepper and fry for 5–6 minutes, stirring frequently, until softened.

Stir in the tomatoes, rice and saffron and pour in the stock. Season with salt and plenty of black pepper. Cover and cook over gentle heat for about 20 minutes, or until the rice is almost tender, adding a little more stock if necessary.

Stir in the mixed seafood and chicken and cook for 5 minutes, or until the rice is just tender and all the liquid has been absorbed.

Break the eggs into a large bowl, add salt and pepper and whisk briefly with a fork. Stir in the paella mixture and the peas into the eggs.

Wipe out the pan with kitchen paper. Heat the remaining oil in the pan over medium heat. Add the tortilla mixture and cook over medium-low heat for 10–15 minutes, or until almost set.

Slide under a preheated grill to set the top. Leave to stand for 5 minutes, then transfer to a serving plate and serve, cut into wedges.

* If ready-mixed seafood cocktail is unavailable, use 50 g each of shelled prawns, shelled mussels and squid rings.

Chickpeas are a delicious alternative to potatoes in a tortilla, adding a slightly sweet, nutty flavour. This tortilla is quite filling, so is best as a main meal, served with a green salad.

chickpea tortilla

Break the eggs into a large bowl, add the paprika, salt, and pepper and whisk briefly with a fork. Stir in the parsley.

Heat 2 tablespoons of the oil in a large non-stick frying pan. Add the onion and red pepper and cook for about 5 minutes until softened, turning frequently. Add the garlic and chickpeas and cook for 2 minutes.

Transfer the chickpea mixture to the bowl of eggs and stir gently. Add the remaining oil to the pan and return to the heat. Add the tortilla mixture, spreading it evenly in the pan. Cook over medium-low heat until the bottom is golden brown and the top almost set.

Put a plate on top of the pan and hold it in place. Invert the pan so the tortilla drops onto the plate. Slide back into the pan, brown side up, and cook for another 2–3 minutes until lightly browned on the other side. Serve hot or at room temperature, cut into wedges.

5 large eggs

½ teaspoon sweet paprika

3 tablespoons freshly chopped flat leaf parsley

3 tablespoons extra virgin olive oil

1 large onion, finely chopped

1 red pepper, halved, deseeded and chopped

2 garlic cloves, finely chopped

400-g tin chickpeas, drained and rinsed

sea salt and freshly ground black pepper

serves 2–3

Most tortillas are inverted onto a plate and returned to the pan to finish cooking. However, this tortilla is topped with cured mountain ham and should be finished under the grill. You can trickle a little extra virgin olive oil over the top before grilling and even add a few slices of goats' cheese log, which melts beautifully into the top of the tortilla.

artichoke & ham tortilla

3 tablespoons extra virgin olive or sunflower oil

3 medium potatoes, about 350 g, peeled and cubed

1 large onion, chopped

5 large eggs

400-g tin artichoke hearts in water, well drained and cut in half

2 tablespoons fresh thyme leaves

100 g thinly sliced serrano ham, torn into strips

6–8 slices goats' cheese log with rind, about 125 g (optional)

sea salt and freshly ground black pepper

serves 3–4

Heat 2 tablespoons of the oil in a large non-stick frying pan. Add the potatoes and cook over medium heat for 5 minutes. Add the onion and cook for a further 10 minutes, lifting and turning occasionally, until just tender. The potatoes and onions should not brown very much.

Meanwhile, break the eggs into a large bowl, season with salt and pepper and whisk briefly with a fork. Add the artichokes, thyme and about three-quarters of the ham. Add the potatoes and onion and stir gently.

Heat the remaining oil in the frying pan. Add the tortilla mixture, spreading it evenly in the pan. Cook over medium-low heat for about 6 minutes, then top with the remaining ham. Cook for a further 4–5 minutes or until the bottom is golden brown and the top almost set.

Add the goats' cheese, if using, and slide under a preheated grill just to brown the top, about 2–3 minutes. Serve hot or warm, cut into wedges.

noodles & stir-fries

Pork fillet is given a spicy, hearty boost with classic Thai flavourings, and the toasted coconut finishes off this super-tasty stir-fry perfectly with a subtle smokiness. If you can't get hold of Thai basil, simply replace with fresh coriander.

thai-flavour pork

Heat a wok or large frying pan and add the coconut when hot. Dry-fry for a few minutes until golden. Remove from the wok and set aside.

Place the pork fillet in between 2 large sheets of clingfilm, then bash with a rolling pin until about 2 cm thick. Slice very thinly. Season the pork with salt and pepper.

Heat the oil in the wok, then brown the pork in 2 or 3 batches, adding more oil if necessary. Remove and set aside.

Add the ginger, garlic, chillies and lemongrass to the wok and stir-fry for 1 minute. Return the pork to the wok and stir-fry for 1 minute. Add the chilli sauce and fish sauce, and stir well. Cook for a further 2 minutes, or until the pork is completely cooked through. Stir through the Thai basil. Remove from the heat and serve immediately with rice or egg noodles with the toasted coconut sprinkled over the top.

4–5 tablespoons grated fresh coconut (or desiccated, if necessary)

600 g pork fillet

2 tablespoons vegetable or groundnut oil

1 teaspoon finely grated fresh ginger

3 cloves garlic, thinly sliced

4 whole fresh bird's-eye chillies

1 stalk lemongrass, outer leaves removed, bottom 6 cm halved and thinly sliced

2 tablespoons chilli sauce

1 tablespoon Thai fish sauce

a large handful of Thai basil

sea salt and freshly ground black pepper

serves 4

Classic Chinese crispy duck is given an updated twist with an aromatic dry rub of five-spice powder, fresh plums and meaty aubergine to soak up the tangy sauce. Serve with either noodles or rice.

five-spice duck

2 skinless duck breasts, thinly sliced

1 teaspoon five-spice powder

2 tablespoons vegetable or groundnut oil

1 medium onion, sliced

1 small aubergine, quartered and sliced

2 plums, stoned and cut into wedges

sea salt and freshly ground black pepper

sauce

3 tablespoons Chinese plum sauce

1 tablespoon rice wine vinegar

2 tablespoons clear honey

1 tablespoon dark soy sauce

serves 2–3

Combine all the ingredients for the sauce in a bowl and set aside.

Place the duck in a bowl and sprinkle over the five-spice powder, a sprinkling of salt and freshly ground pepper. Rub well into the duck.

Heat the oil in a wok or large frying pan. Add the duck in batches and cook until sealed all over. Remove and set aside.

Add the onion to the wok, with a little more oil if necessary, and cook for 2 minutes until softened and golden. Add the aubergine with a good sprinkling of water and stir-fry for 2–3 minutes. Return the duck to the wok and stir well. Add the sauce ingredients, reduce the heat and simmer for a further 3–4 minutes, covered, until the aubergine is just tender.

Remove the lid, then stir in the plum wedges. Cook for 2 minutes, then check the seasoning, adding more salt or soy sauce if necessary. Serve immediately with noodles or rice.

Why order a take-away when you can knock up this fresh-tasting, healthy alternative to the perennial Chinese favourite quickly and easily? Don't worry if you can't find Chinese rice wine; use dry sherry instead. Serve with either noodles or rice.

chinese lemon chicken

To make the marinade, combine all the ingredients in a bowl and mix well. Stir in the chicken, cover and marinate in the fridge for 20–30 minutes.

Meanwhile, to make the sauce, put all the ingredients in a bowl with 2 tablespoons cold water, stir to combine and set aside.

Heat a wok or large frying pan. When hot, add the sesame seeds and dry-fry over medium heat for about 2 minutes, or until lightly toasted. Remove from the heat and set aside.

When you are ready to cook the chicken, heat 1½ tablespoons of the oil in the wok until very hot. Add half the marinated chicken and stir-fry for 3–4 minutes until golden brown and well sealed all over. Spoon out into a dish and repeat with the remaining chicken. Set aside.

Add the remaining oil to the wok and add the onion. Stir-fry for 2–3 minutes until softened and golden. Pour in the sauce and bring to the boil, then reduce the heat and simmer for 1 minute.

Return the chicken to the wok and stir through the sauce. Simmer for 2 minutes, or until the chicken is cooked through. Remove from the heat. Serve immediately over noodles or rice with the toasted sesame seeds sprinkled over the top and garnished with the sliced spring onions.

4 skinless chicken breasts, cut into thin strips

1 tablespoon sesame seeds

2 tablespoons groundnut or vegetable oil

1 onion, thinly sliced

2 spring onions, green parts only, thinly sliced on the diagonal, to garnish

marinade

1 tablespoon light soy sauce

1 tablespoon Chinese rice wine

2 teaspoons finely grated fresh ginger

2 garlic cloves, crushed

1 teaspoon cornflour

sauce

80 ml chicken stock

freshly squeezed juice and finely grated zest from 1 large unwaxed lemon

3 tablespoons clear honey

1 tablespoon light soy sauce

1 teaspoon sesame oil

2 teaspoons cornflour

serves 4

Transform everyday vegetables into a memorable meal with a few carefully chosen whole and ground spices. As in many Indian-influenced dishes, a spiky ginger and garlic paste forms the basis of this stir-fry – why not make extra and store in the fridge or freezer for another day? Serve with either basmati or white long grain rice.

spiced mixed vegetables

1 teaspoon finely grated fresh ginger

2 cloves garlic, chopped

1 tablespoon vegetable oil

½ teaspoon fennel seeds

1 teaspoon cumin seeds

1 onion, halved and sliced

¼ teaspoon ground cumin

¼ teaspoon ground coriander

½ teaspoon chilli powder

150 g tinned chopped tomatoes

200 g cauliflower, cut into small florets

120 g carrots, peeled and cut into batons

120 g green beans, sliced on the diagonal into 3-cm pieces

2 tablespoons freshly chopped coriander

sea salt

serves 2

Place the ginger and garlic in a blender and whiz to a paste with a touch of water. Alternatively, pound to a paste with a pestle and mortar.

Heat the oil in a wok or large frying pan and add the fennel and cumin seeds and stir until they start to pop. Add the onion and cook for a further 3–4 minutes until golden. Stir in the ginger and garlic paste and continue to cook for a further 2 minutes, stirring. Spoon in the ground cumin, ground coriander and chilli powder and, after a few seconds, the tomatoes. Cook briskly for 1 minute until most of the liquid has evaporated.

Add the cauliflower and carrots to the wok with a good sprinkle of water, stir, then cover immediately and cook for 2 minutes.

Add the green beans, season with salt and cook for a further 2–3 minutes uncovered until the vegetables are cooked but still a little crunchy. Taste and add more salt if necessary.

Remove from the heat and stir in the coriander leaves. Serve immediately with rice.

Ideal for quick and casual entertaining, this stir-fry has the deliciously different savoury taste of yellow bean sauce and the colourful combination of red and yellow peppers. Rice or noodles, tossed with a little sesame oil, is the ideal accompaniment to this dish.

chicken & yellow bean stir-fry

Combine all the marinade ingredients in a bowl, then add the chicken pieces and mix well. Leave to marinate in the fridge for 10–15 minutes.

When ready to cook, heat the oil in a wok or large frying pan. When hot, add the chicken and stir-fry for 3–4 minutes until golden, well sealed and nearly cooked through. Remove from the wok and set aside.

Add the peppers to the wok and stir-fry briskly over high heat for 2 minutes. Return the chicken to the wok and add the yellow bean sauce. Cook for another minute, stirring occasionally.

Meanwhile, combine the soy sauce, chicken stock and cornflour in a bowl with 2 tablespoons cold water. Stir until smooth, then pour into the wok. Simmer gently until the sauce has thickened and the chicken is cooked through. Remove from the heat and sprinkle with the almonds, if using. Serve immediately with rice or noodles tossed with a little sesame oil.

2 large skinless chicken breasts, cut into 2-cm chunks

1 tablespoon groundnut oil

1 red and 1 yellow pepper, deseeded and thinly sliced

2 tablespoons Chinese yellow bean sauce

½ tablespoon light soy sauce

70 ml chicken stock

2 teaspoons cornflour

1 tablespoon lightly toasted flaked almonds, to garnish (optional)

marinade

½ tablespoon Chinese rice wine or dry sherry

1 tablespoon light soy sauce

1 teaspoon sesame oil

½ teaspoon sugar

1 teaspoon finely grated fresh ginger

a pinch of dried chilli flakes

serves 2

The fat and chewy wheat-based Japanese udon noodles make this dish wonderfully satisfying. The richly flavoured gravy gets its complex undertones from a good dose of oyster sauce, and the tofu and meaty shitake mushrooms absorb it completely for a thoroughly tasty dish.

tofu & mushroom noodles

400 g udon noodles

1 tablespoon vegetable or groundnut oil

300 g firm tofu, cut into 2-cm cubes

1 teaspoon finely grated fresh ginger

3 spring onions, white and light green parts cut into 2-cm lengths and shredded; green parts sliced on the diagonal

1 red chilli, deseeded and thinly shredded

200 g shitake mushrooms, caps sliced, stalks discarded

sauce

2 tablespoons oyster sauce

1 tablespoon light soy sauce

150 ml vegetable stock

1 tablespoon cornflour combined with 2 tablespoons cold water

serves 2

Bring a saucepan of water to the boil. Add the udon noodles and cook according to the packet instructions. Drain and rinse under cold running water. Set aside.

To make the sauce, combine all the ingredients in a measuring jug. Set aside.

Heat the oil in a wok or large frying pan. When hot, add the tofu. Cook, stirring gently, until golden all over. Remove the tofu from the wok, and drain on kitchen paper.

Add the ginger, shredded spring onion and chilli to the wok, and stir-fry for 1 minute over high heat. Add the mushrooms and cook for 1 more minute, then pour in the sauce and bring to the boil. Reduce the heat, return the tofu to the wok and simmer gently for 1–2 minutes until the sauce thickens.

Stir the cooked and drained noodles into the sauce very carefully and heat through. Remove from the heat, garnish with the remaining spring onion and serve immediately.

Thai food always presents the palate with a kaleidoscope of flavours and the knack is getting the balance just right. Pad thai needs to be really sweet and soothing, but the tamarind and lime give it a fruity tang of sourness and the fish sauce provides a characteristic salty depth.

pad thai

Soak the noodles according to the instructions on the packet, then drain and shake dry. Set aside. Combine the tamarind paste, fish sauce and sugar and set aside.

Heat the oil in a wok or large frying pan over medium heat and add the garlic. Stir-fry until the garlic begins to colour, then add the prawns, peanuts and chilli flakes. Stir-fry for another 2–3 minutes, or until the prawns turn pink and the nuts are golden.

Add the noodles to the wok along with the tamarind mixture. Toss until everything is evenly coated and push to one side of the wok. Pour the egg into a corner of the wok and cook until it is scrambled and dry, then stir into the noodle mixture. Add the beansprouts and spring onions, give it one final toss and transfer to bowls. Serve with a few lime wedges on the side.

200 g flat medium rice noodles

2 tablespoons tamarind paste

3 tablespoons Thai fish sauce

3 tablespoons palm sugar or demerara sugar

2 tablespoons sunflower oil

3 garlic cloves, crushed

250 g uncooked tiger prawns, shelled and deveined but tails intact

50 g unsalted peanuts, chopped

½ teaspoon dried chilli flakes

2 eggs, beaten

150 g beansprouts

4 spring onions, shredded

lime wedges, to serve

serves 2

Most noodle dishes take just a matter of minutes to cook –
in fact, noodles made of rice flour or mung bean starch are
ready almost instantly. Wheat-based noodles take the most
time – but even then, only about the same as regular pasta.

gingered chicken noodles

2 tablespoons rice wine

2 teaspoons cornflour

350 g skinless chicken breasts

175 g Chinese dried egg noodles

3 tablespoons groundnut or
sunflower oil

3 cm fresh ginger, peeled and
thinly sliced

125 g mangetout, thinly sliced

4 tablespoons freshly chopped
chives

125 g cashew nuts, toasted in
a dry frying pan, then chopped

sauce

100 ml chicken stock

2 tablespoons dark soy sauce

1 tablespoon freshly squeezed
lemon juice

1 tablespoon sesame oil

2 teaspoons soft brown sugar

serves 4

Put the rice wine and cornflour into a bowl and mix well. Cut the
chicken into small chunks, add to the bowl, stir well and set aside
to marinate while you prepare the remaining ingredients.

Prepare the noodles according to the instructions on the packet, then
drain and shake dry.

Put all the sauce ingredients into a small bowl and mix well.

Heat half the oil in a wok or large frying pan, then add the chicken and
stir-fry for 2 minutes until golden. Remove to a plate and wipe the wok
clean with kitchen paper. Add the remaining oil, then the ginger and
mangetout, and fry for 1 minute. Return the chicken to the wok, then
add the noodles and sauce. Heat through for 2 minutes.

Add the chives and cashew nuts, stir well and serve.

To lift your stir-fries out of the ordinary and into the sublime, you need to be a little crafty with ingredients. Both lemongrass and kaffir lime leaves can be difficult to find, but they freeze well, so keep a few in the freezer for meals such as this. Serve with either steamed rice or egg noodles.

stir-fried asparagus & tofu

Heat the oil in a wok or large frying pan over medium/low heat and add the cashew nuts, chillies, lemongrass, lime leaves, garlic and ginger. Gently fry for 1 minute.

Add the tofu, asparagus and red peppers and stir-fry for a further 2 minutes until they start to soften around the edges and the cashew nuts turn golden.

Add the tamarind paste, soy sauce and honey, along with 100 ml water and turn up the heat to bring the liquid to the boil. Allow the contents of the wok to bubble up so that the liquid finishes cooking the vegetables. This should take a further 3 minutes or so.

Transfer to bowls. Remove the slices of ginger, unless you like a very feisty flavour! Serve piping hot with steamed rice or egg noodles.

1 tablespoon sunflower oil

50 g cashew nuts

2 large red chillies, sliced (and deseeded if you prefer it mild)

1 lemongrass stalk (outer layer discarded), finely chopped

2 kaffir lime leaves, shredded

2 garlic cloves, crushed

2 cm fresh ginger, sliced

250 g silken tofu, cubed

250 g medium asparagus tips

2 red peppers, cut into strips

1 tablespoon tamarind paste

2 tablespoons dark soy sauce

1 tablespoon clear honey

serves 4

risottos & paellas

Smoky chargrilled artichokes are wonderful combined with nutty pecorino. Pecorino is made from ewes' milk, and when aged can be grated like Parmesan. When young, it has a Cheddar-like texture and a rich, nutty flavour.

artichoke & pecorino risotto

Cut the artichokes into quarters and set aside.

Melt half the butter in a large, heavy saucepan and add the onion. Cook gently for 10 minutes until soft, golden and translucent but not browned. Add the rice and stir until well coated with the butter and heated through. Pour in the wine and boil hard until it has reduced and almost disappeared. This will remove the taste of raw alcohol.

Begin adding the stock, a large ladle at a time, stirring gently until each ladle has almost been absorbed by the rice. The risotto should be kept at a bare simmer throughout cooking, so don't let the rice dry out – add more stock as necessary. Continue until the rice is tender and creamy, but the grains still firm. (This should take 15–20 minutes depending on the type of rice used – check the packet instructions.)

Taste and season well with salt and pepper and beat in the remaining butter and all the pecorino. Fold in the artichokes. Cover and leave to rest for a couple of minutes, then serve immediately. You may like to add a little more hot stock to the risotto just before you serve to loosen it, but don't let it wait around too long or the rice will turn mushy.

12 chargrilled deli artichokes

125 g unsalted butter

1 onion, finely chopped

500 g risotto rice

150 ml dry white wine

about 1.5 litres hot vegetable stock or chicken stock

75 g freshly grated pecorino cheese

sea salt and freshly ground black pepper

serves 4–6

A wonderfully light and fragrant risotto, perfect for the summer, to serve with cold chicken or fish. Try to use the more fragrant soft herbs here – the more, the merrier.

green herb risotto

125 g unsalted butter

8 spring onions, green and white parts, finely chopped

150 ml dry white wine

finely grated zest and freshly squeezed juice of 1 large unwaxed lemon

500 g risotto rice

about 1.5 litres hot vegetable stock or chicken stock

4 tablespoons freshly chopped herbs such as parsley, basil, marjoram and thyme

75 g freshly grated Parmesan cheese

sea salt and freshly ground black pepper

serves 4–6

Melt half the butter in a large, heavy saucepan and add the spring onions. Cook gently for 3–5 minutes until soft. Pour in the wine, add half the lemon zest and boil hard until the wine has reduced and almost disappeared. This will remove the taste of raw alcohol. Add the rice and stir until well coated with butter and onions and heated through.

Begin to add the hot stock, a large ladle at a time, stirring until each ladle has been absorbed by the rice. Continue until the rice is tender and creamy, but the grains still firm. (This should take 15–20 minutes depending on the type of rice used – check the packet instructions.)

Taste and season well with salt and lots of freshly ground black pepper. Stir in the remaining butter, the lemon zest, juice, herbs and Parmesan. Cover and leave to rest for a couple of minutes, then serve immediately.

A pretty, delicate risotto made even more special with sliced courgette flowers. The female flowers will produce a courgette if fertilized, while the male flowers are the ones used for stuffing. They are just a flower on a stalk and the central spike must be removed before cooking. Courgette flowers are sold in Italian greengrocers and farmers' markets.

courgette flower risotto

Melt half the butter in a large, heavy saucepan and add the onion and celery. Cook gently for 10 minutes until soft, golden and translucent but not browned. Add the rice and stir until well coated with the butter and heated through.

Begin adding the stock, a large ladle at a time, stirring gently until each ladle has almost been absorbed by the rice. The risotto should be kept at a bare simmer throughout cooking, so don't let the rice dry out – add more stock as necessary. Halfway through cooking, stir in the courgettes. Continue cooking and adding stock until the rice is tender and creamy, but the grains still firm. (This should take 15–20 minutes, depending on the type of rice used – check the packet instructions.)

Taste and season well with salt and pepper, beat in the remaining butter and all the Parmesan, then stir in the courgette flowers. Cover and leave to rest for a couple of minutes, then serve immediately. You may like to add a little more hot stock to the risotto just before you serve to loosen it, but don't let it wait around too long or the rice will turn mushy.

125 g unsalted butter

1 onion, finely chopped

1 celery stick, finely chopped

400 g risotto rice

about 1.5 litres hot vegetable stock or chicken stock

4 courgettes, grated

50 g freshly grated Parmesan cheese

4–6 courgette flowers, trimmed and thinly sliced

sea salt and freshly ground black pepper

serves 4

Any kind of fresh wild mushroom will make this risotto taste wonderful – black trompettes des morts, deep golden girolles or musky chanterelles.

wild mushroom risotto

125 g unsalted butter

1 large onion, finely chopped

2 garlic cloves, finely chopped

250 g mixed wild mushrooms, cleaned and coarsely chopped

1 tablespoon chopped fresh thyme

1 tablespoon chopped fresh marjoram

150 ml dry white wine or vermouth

500 g risotto rice

about 1.5 litres hot vegetable stock or chicken stock

75 g freshly grated Parmesan cheese, plus extra to serve

sea salt and freshly ground black pepper

serves 4–6

Melt half the butter in a large, heavy saucepan and add the onion and garlic. Cook gently for 10 minutes until soft, golden and translucent but not browned. Stir in the mushrooms and herbs, then cook over medium heat for 3 minutes to heat through. Pour in the wine and boil hard until it has reduced and almost disappeared. This will remove the taste of raw alcohol. Stir in the rice and fry with the onion and mushrooms until dry and slightly opaque.

Begin adding the hot stock, a large ladle at a time, stirring until each ladle has been absorbed by the rice. Continue until the rice is tender and creamy, but the grains still firm. (This should take 15–20 minutes depending on the type of rice used – check the packet instructions.)

Taste and season well with salt and pepper. Stir in the remaining butter and the Parmesan, cover and leave to rest for a couple of minutes. Serve immediately with extra grated Parmesan. You may like to add a little more hot stock to the risotto just before you serve to loosen it, but don't let it wait around too long or the rice will turn mushy.

Salad leaves, herbs and bulghur wheat are combined here with chickpeas in a variation of this Middle Eastern dish. When buying salad leaves, keep in mind you will need about two large handfuls per person. If they wilt a little on the way home, give them a quick bath in a bowl of cold water with a pinch or two of sugar thrown in, to freshen them up.

tabbouleh with chickpeas

Put the bulghur wheat in a heatproof bowl and pour over 125 ml boiling water. Stir once, cover tightly with clingfilm and set aside for 8–10 minutes. Put the lemon juice and oil in a small bowl and whisk. Pour over the bulghur and stir well with a fork, fluffing up the bulghur and separating the grains.

Put the bulghur in a large bowl with the parsley, mint, dill, tomatoes, chickpeas and salad leaves. Use your hands to toss everything together. Season well with salt and pepper. Transfer to a serving plate and serve with toasted Turkish bread, if you like.

90 g bulghur wheat

2 tablespoons freshly squeezed lemon juice

60 ml extra virgin olive oil

1 small bunch of flat leaf parsley, finely chopped

1 large handful of mint leaves, finely chopped

2 tablespoons finely chopped dill

1 small punnet of cherry tomatoes, halved

400-g tin chickpeas, drained and rinsed

120–150 g mixed salad leaves

sea salt and freshly ground black pepper

toasted Turkish flat bread, to serve (optional)

serves 4

This spicy prawn dish couldn't be any quicker or simpler to make, and it can even be prepared in advance. On the day, all you need do is make the couscous.

prawns with couscous

4 tablespoons extra virgin olive oil

2 teaspoons ground cumin

1 teaspoon ground ginger

1 teaspoon paprika

½ teaspoon cayenne pepper

1 kg medium uncooked prawns, peeled

2 garlic cloves, crushed

2 lemons, 1 juiced, 1 cut into wedges for serving

a bunch of fresh coriander, leaves finely chopped

sea salt and freshly ground black pepper

couscous

250 g couscous

½ teaspoon sea salt

3–4 tablespoons extra virgin olive oil

freshly squeezed juice of ½ lemon

serves 4

To prepare the couscous, pour it into a large bowl, add the salt and mix. Add 400 ml boiling water and 1 tablespoon oil. Cover and set aside for about 5 minutes to absorb the water.

Using your fingers, break up the lumps of couscous to air them. Fluff up with a fork and set aside while you make the prawns.

Heat the oil in a frying pan. Add the cumin, ginger, paprika and cayenne and cook, stirring, for 30 seconds. Add the prawns, garlic and a good pinch of salt. Cook, stirring, for 1 minute. Add the juice of 1 lemon and 250 ml water. Stir, then cover and simmer until the prawns are opaque and cooked through, for 3–5 minutes. Remove from the heat and stir in the coriander. Taste and adjust the seasoning with salt, pepper and extra lemon juice if necessary.

Transfer the couscous to a serving plate and season with the juice of ½ lemon and 2–3 tablespoons oil. Stir well. Put the prawns on top, sprinkle with their cooking juices and serve with the lemon wedges.

This dish of jasmine rice and tinned crabmeat, with the addition of a few fresh ingredients, is a truly luxurious feast. If you are really looking to impress, then use freshly picked white crabmeat, but go easy on the flavourings, as you don't want to overwhelm the delicate sweetness of the crab.

jasmine rice with crab & asparagus

Heat the oil in a wok or large frying pan. When hot, add the onion and stir-fry over high heat for 2–3 minutes, or until softened and golden. Add the garlic and chilli and cook for a further minute. Add the asparagus stalks and stir-fry for 2 minutes, then add the tips and 2 teaspoons of the soy sauce and fry for 30 seconds. Stir in the crabmeat and heat through.

Mix in the rice, then pour over the chilli sauce, remaining soy sauce and sesame oil. Stir well until everything is thoroughly combined and the rice is piping hot. Taste and check for seasoning, then stir in the chives and remove from the heat. Serve immediately.

1 tablespoon groundnut oil

1 small onion, finely chopped

2 garlic cloves, crushed

1 large red chilli, deseeded and finely chopped

130 g fine asparagus, cut into 2-cm pieces, tips and stalks kept separately

2 teaspoons light soy sauce, plus extra if needed

200 g tinned or fresh white crabmeat, well drained

250 g cooked jasmine rice

1 tablespoon sweet chilli sauce

¼ teaspoon toasted sesame oil

2 tablespoons snipped chives

serves 2

Paella is made in countless variations in different areas of Spain, depending on local ingredients and styles. Traditional combinations include rabbit with snails, and pork ribs with cauliflower and beans, and an all-vegetable paella is also popular these days. Don't stir paella constantly like risotto.

chicken & pork paella

8 chicken drumsticks and thighs, mixed, or 1 whole chicken, about 1.5 kg, cut into pieces

2 teaspoons sea salt

freshly ground black pepper

4 teaspoons paprika

4 tablespoons extra virgin olive oil

3–4 boneless pork chops, or 325 g salt pork cut into 3-cm cubes

2 onions, chopped

4 garlic cloves, crushed

500 g tomatoes, fresh or tinned, skinned, deseeded and chopped

2 large pinches of saffron threads

350 g paella rice

750–800 ml hot chicken stock or vegetable stock

100 g frozen peas, thawed

200 g green beans, halved

8 baby artichokes, halved lengthways, or tinned or marinated equivalent

8 large uncooked prawns, shells on

serves 4–6

Pat the chicken dry with kitchen paper. Put 1 teaspoon each of salt, pepper and paprika in a bowl and mix well. Sprinkle the chicken with half the mixture and toss well.

Heat the oil in a large, shallow frying pan. Add the chicken and pork, in batches if necessary, and fry over medium heat for 10–12 minutes or until well browned. Remove with a slotted spoon and set aside.

Add the onions, garlic, tomatoes and saffron to the pan, then add the remaining salt and paprika. Cook until thickened, about 5 minutes. Stir the mixture well, then replace the meats, stir in the rice and most of the hot stock. Cook over high heat until bubbling fiercely, then reduce the heat and simmer gently, uncovered, for 15 minutes.

Add the peas, beans, artichokes, prawns and remaining stock, if necessary, and continue to cook for 10–15 minutes more or until the rice is cooked and glossy but dry. Serve the paella straight from the pan.

This technique of cooking rice is Middle Eastern in origin but it has spread far and wide – similar rice dishes can be found in European, Asian, Latin American, Caribbean and Indian cuisines, and it is known by many names, including pilau, pilav and pulao.

orange vegetable pilaf

Put the oil in a heavy-based saucepan set over high heat. Add the onion, garlic, ginger and chilli and cook for 5 minutes, stirring often. Add the spices and almonds and cook for a further 5 minutes, until the spices become aromatic and look very dark in the pan.

Add the rice and cook for a minute, stirring well to coat the rice in the spices. Add the carrot, pumpkin and sweet potato to the pan. Pour in 600 ml water and stir well, loosening any grains of rice that are stuck to the bottom of the pan. Bring to the boil, then reduce the heat to low, cover the pan with a tight-fitting lid and cook for 25 minutes, stirring occasionally.

Add the lime juice and coriander, stir well to combine, and serve.

2 tablespoons olive oil

1 onion, chopped

2 garlic cloves, chopped

1 tablespoon finely grated fresh ginger

1 large red chilli, finely chopped

1 teaspoon ground coriander

1 teaspoon ground cumin

1 teaspoon turmeric

50 g flaked almonds

300 g basmati rice

1 carrot, cut into large chunks

200 g pumpkin or squash, peeled, deseeded and cut into wedges

1 small sweet potato, peeled and cut into thick half-circles

freshly squeezed juice of 1 lime

1 handful of freshly chopped coriander

serves 4

This vegetarian take on a classic Spanish paella is colourful, delicious and bursting with fresh, young summer vegetables grown on the vine and enhanced with the subtle flavour of saffron. Perfect for summer entertaining.

vegetarian paella

a large pinch of saffron threads

80 ml olive oil

200 g red or yellow cherry tomatoes

100 g green beans

4 baby courgettes, halved

80 g frozen peas, thawed

2 garlic cloves, chopped

2 fresh rosemary sprigs

320 g paella rice

800 ml vegetable stock

30 g flaked almonds, lightly toasted

serves 4

Put the saffron in a bowl with 65 ml hot water and set aside to infuse. Heat half of the oil in a heavy-based frying pan set over high heat and add the tomatoes. Cook for 2 minutes, shaking the pan so that the tomatoes soften and start to split. Remove the tomatoes from the pan with a slotted spoon and set aside. Add the beans, courgettes and peas and stir-fry over high heat for 2–3 minutes. Set aside with the tomatoes.

Add the remaining oil to the pan with the garlic and rosemary, and cook gently for 1 minute to flavour the oil. Add the stock and saffron water to the pan, then stir in the rice. Cook over high heat until bubbling fiercely, then reduce the heat and simmer gently, uncovered, for about 20 minutes until almost all the stock has been absorbed.

Scatter the cooked tomatoes, beans, courgettes and peas over the rice, cover lightly with some foil and cook over low heat for 5 minutes so that the vegetables are just heated through. Sprinkle the almonds on top to serve.

This vegetarian dish comes from Valencia, where it is served during the Lenten fast. Its Spanish name – arroz al horno con perdiz – means 'rice with partridge', although the partridge is really a whole bulb of garlic.

baked rice with garlic

Preheat the oven to 180°C (350°F) Gas 4.

Heat the oil in a heatproof shallow casserole or frying pan with an ovenproof handle. Add the garlic bulb and onion and fry for 12 minutes over low heat until the garlic is pale golden and beginning to soften and the onion soft and golden.

Remove the garlic and reserve. Increase the heat and add the tomatoes and juices. Cook until the mixture starts to thicken a little. Stir in the paprika, and salt and pepper to taste.

Stir in the rice. Add half the stock or water and bring slowly to the boil. Add the chickpeas, drain the raisins and gently fold them into the rice. Put the garlic in the centre and bake in the preheated oven for 10 minutes. Heat the remaining stock or water, then add as much as the rice seems to need. Continue baking for 10–15 minutes before serving, covering the top with foil if it seems to be over-browning or drying out. Serve from the casserole.

100 ml olive oil

1 garlic bulb, left whole, skin on

1 large onion, finely chopped

4 tomatoes, skinned, deseeded and chopped (keep the juices)

1 teaspoon sweet paprika

450 g paella rice

up to 1 litre vegetable stock or water

400-g tin chickpeas, drained and rinsed

50 g raisins, soaked in hot water for 30 minutes until plump

sea salt and freshly ground black pepper

serves 6

This makes a great mid-week supper dish. Feel free to increase your vegetable intake by adding vegetables of your choice. Frozen peas, corn kernels or green beans are particularly useful, as they cook in minutes and don't require any preparation.

1 tablespoon olive oil

200 g basmati rice

1 large onion, chopped

1 teaspoon ground turmeric

400-g tin chopped tomatoes

1 large red pepper, deseeded and finely chopped

1–2 garlic cloves, chopped

500 ml chicken stock

400-g tin butter beans, drained and rinsed

1–2 red chillies, deseeded and thinly sliced

500 g cooked peeled prawns, thawed if frozen

3 tablespoons fresh coriander, coarsely chopped

sea salt and freshly ground black pepper

serves 4

prawn & butter bean rice

Heat the oil in a large non-stick saucepan. Add the rice, onion and turmeric and cook over medium heat, stirring, for 2 minutes. Add the tomatoes, pepper, garlic, stock and salt and pepper, to taste. Cover the pan with a tight-fitting lid, reduce the heat and simmer for 15 minutes, until most of the stock has been absorbed by the rice.

Add the butter beans, chillies and prawns to the rice mixture and stir through gently. Replace the lid and cook for a further 3 minutes, or until the stock is absorbed and the prawns are thoroughly warmed through. Stir in the coriander and serve immediately.

Variation Brown four skinned, boneless chicken thighs in the oil, then add to the rice and onion and proceed as above. Add some frozen peas and corn kernels with the butter beans and prawns and cook for 3–5 minutes or until cooked and piping hot. Serve with lemon wedges, if you like.

This protein-packed salad is ideal for lunch. It uses brown basmati rice, which releases its sugars into the bloodstream at a very slow rate throughout the afternoon.

saffron fish pilaf

Heat the oil in a large frying pan, add the onion and garlic, if using, and fry gently for 3 minutes. Add the rice and continue to fry, stirring, for 2 minutes. Add the saffron powder and stir well. Pour in half the stock, bring to the boil, then reduce the heat and simmer gently for 25 minutes, stirring occasionally, adding more stock as it is absorbed by the rice.

Add the fish, peas, sweetcorn and tomatoes, stir well and cook for a further 5–10 minutes. Add the coriander and black pepper, to taste, then cook for 5 minutes more until the rice is tender.

Top with the hard-boiled egg, then serve.

Variation Replace the fish with 300 g chopped ham and 100 g chopped fresh pineapple.

2 teaspoons olive oil

1 onion, chopped

2–3 garlic cloves, crushed (optional)

175 g brown basmati rice, rinsed

¼ teaspoon saffron powder

750–900 ml vegetable stock

350 g white fish, such as cod fillet, skinned if necessary and cut into small pieces

100 g undyed smoked haddock fillet, skinned and cut into small pieces (optional)

50 g frozen peas

50 g frozen sweetcorn kernels

225 g tomatoes, chopped

1 tablespoon freshly chopped coriander

2 hard-boiled eggs, shelled and quartered

freshly ground black pepper

serves 4–6

This pilaf is typical of many Middle Eastern dishes that combine dried fruit and nuts as well as grains and meat. The sultanas and dried apricots give an underlying sweetness to the dish.

lamb pilaf

Heat 1 tablespoon of the oil in a large frying pan, add the onion and garlic and fry for 5 minutes. Add the cardamom, cinnamon, bay leaves and almonds and cook for a further 4 minutes. Transfer to a plate.

Heat the remaining oil and fry the lamb on high heat until browned all over. Return the onion mixture to the pan along with the sultanas and apricots. Pour in just enough water to cover, then bring to the boil, cover and simmer for 1½ hours.

Add the rice, stir well and cover with water. Bring to the boil, then cover and simmer very gently for 30 minutes. Add the parsley, if liked, and serve.

3 tablespoons olive oil

1 onion, chopped

2 garlic cloves, crushed

5 cardamom pods, crushed

1 cinnamon stick

3 bay leaves

50 g blanched almonds

500 g lamb neck fillet, cut into 3-cm pieces

50 g sultanas

50 g dried apricots

300 g basmati rice

a handful of freshly chopped parsley (optional)

serves 4

curries & tagines

A tagine is a Moroccan stew as well as the earthenware pot in which the dish is traditionally cooked. The stew is usually made with either meat or poultry, gently simmered with vegetables, olives, preserved lemons, garlic and spices.

chicken & olive tagine

In a bowl, mix together all the ingredients for the marinade. Put the chicken thighs or legs in a shallow dish and coat them in the marinade, rubbing it into the skin. Cover and chill in the fridge for 1–2 hours.

Heat the olive oil with the butter in a tagine or heavy-based casserole. Remove the chicken pieces from the marinade and brown them in the oil. Pour over the marinade that is left in the dish and add enough water to come halfway up the sides of the chicken pieces. Bring to the boil, reduce the heat, cover with a lid and simmer for about 45 minutes, turning the chicken from time to time.

Add the preserved lemon, olives and half the thyme to the tagine. Cover again and simmer for a further 15–20 minutes. Check the seasoning and sprinkle the rest of the thyme over the top. Serve immediately from the tagine.

8–10 chicken thighs or 4 whole legs

1 tablespoon olive oil

a knob of unsalted butter

2 preserved lemons, cut into strips

175 g cracked green olives

1–2 teaspoons dried thyme or oregano

sea salt and freshly ground black pepper

marinade

1 onion, grated

3 garlic cloves, crushed

25 g fresh ginger, peeled and grated

a small bunch of fresh coriander, finely chopped

a pinch of saffron threads

freshly squeezed juice of 1 lemon

1 teaspoon sea salt

3–4 tablespoons olive oil

serves 4

The rosemary and ginger of this spicy and fruity tagine give it a delightful aroma. It can be made with chicken joints or pigeon breasts, pheasant or duck, and needs only a buttery couscous and a leafy salad as an accompaniment.

spicy chicken tagine

2 tablespoons olive oil

a knob of unsalted butter

1 onion, finely chopped

3 sprigs of rosemary, 1 finely chopped, the other 2 cut in half

40 g fresh ginger, peeled and finely chopped

2 red chillies, deseeded and finely chopped

1–2 cinnamon sticks

8 chicken thighs

175 g dried apricots

2 tablespoons clear honey

400-g tin plum tomatoes with their juice

sea salt and freshly ground black pepper

a small bunch of fresh green or purple basil leaves, the larger leaves shredded

serves 4

Heat the oil and butter in a tagine or heavy-based casserole. Stir in the onion, chopped rosemary, ginger and chillies and fry gently until the onion begins to soften.

Stir in the halved rosemary sprigs and the cinnamon sticks. Add the chicken thighs and brown them on both sides. Toss in the apricots with the honey, then stir in the tomatoes with their juice. (Add a little water, if necessary, to ensure there is enough liquid to cover the base of the tagine and submerge the apricots.) Bring the liquid to the boil, then reduce the heat. Cover with a lid and cook gently for 35–40 minutes.

Season to taste with salt and pepper. Sprinkle the basil over the chicken and serve the dish immediately with couscous and a leafy salad.

Summer tagines using seasonal vegetables are often quite light and colourful. Other vegetables that might be added to this recipe include tomatoes, aubergines and peas. This dish is particularly good served with wedges of lemon to squeeze over it and a fresh green salad of young beet, spinach and lettuce leaves.

summer tagine of lamb

Heat the oil in a tagine or heavy-based casserole. Stir in the onion, garlic, cumin and coriander seeds, dried mint and ginger. Once the onions begin to soften, toss in the meat and pour in enough water to just cover it. Bring the water to the boil, reduce the heat, cover with a lid and cook gently for about 1½ hours.

Season the cooking juices with salt and pepper. Add the courgettes, pepper and tomatoes, tucking them around the meat (add a little more water if necessary). Cover with a lid and cook for about 15 minutes, until the courgettes and pepper are cooked but retain a bite.

Toss in some of the parsley and fresh mint, sprinkle the rest over the top and serve immediately with lemon wedges and a green salad.

3–4 tablespoons olive oil

1 onion, roughly chopped

4 garlic cloves, roughly chopped

1 teaspoon cumin seeds

1 teaspoon coriander seeds

1 teaspoon dried mint

25 g fresh ginger, peeled and finely chopped

750 g lean lamb, cut into bite-sized pieces

2 small courgettes, sliced thickly on the diagonal

1 red or green pepper, deseeded and cut into thick strips

4 tomatoes, skinned, deseeded and cut into chunks

a small bunch of fresh flat leaf parsley, roughly chopped

a small bunch of fresh mint leaves, roughly chopped

sea salt and freshly ground black pepper

1 lemon, cut into quarters, to serve

serves 4–6

Shoulder of lamb suits this sweet, spicy tagine perfectly, because it is one of the sweeter cuts of meat. Like all stews made with aromatic spices, it tastes even better the next day, once the flavours have mingled. Serve with couscous.

lamb & broad bean tagine

1.25 kg boneless shoulder of lamb or shoulder chops, cut into large chunks

2 teaspoons ground cinnamon

2 teaspoons ground cumin

½ teaspoon hot chilli powder

1 teaspoon ground turmeric

a pinch of saffron threads

½ teaspoon ground white pepper

2 tablespoons olive oil

3 onions, chopped

3 garlic cloves, peeled and crushed

600 ml hot lamb stock

150 g dates, pitted

200 g broad beans, podded

sea salt

fresh coriander, to garnish

serves 4

Put the lamb in a large bowl and toss with the cinnamon, cumin, chilli powder, turmeric, saffron and white pepper. Heat 1 tablespoon oil in a tagine or heavy-based casserole over high heat, then add half the lamb. Cook for a few minutes, stirring occasionally, until the lamb is evenly browned. Tip into a bowl, add the rest of the oil to the tagine dish and brown the remainder of the lamb. Put all the lamb back in with the onions, garlic, stock and a large pinch of salt. Bring the mixture to the boil, cover with a lid and reduce the heat. Simmer gently for 1 hour.

Add the dates to the tagine and simmer for a further 20 minutes.

Add the broad beans and simmer for a further 10 minutes. The tagine should have been cooking for 1½ hours and the meat should be so tender that it falls apart easily. Garnish with coriander and serve with buttered couscous.

This vegetarian tagine is best made with baby aubergines, but you can also use slender, larger aubergines cut into quarters lengthways. As a main dish, it is delicious served with couscous or bulghur wheat, and a dollop of thick, creamy yoghurt. It can also be served as a side dish to accompany meat or poultry.

tagine of baby aubergines

Heat the oil and butter in a tagine or heavy-based casserole. Stir in the onions and garlic and fry gently until they begin to colour. Add the chillies, the coriander and cumin seeds and the sugar. When the seeds give off a nutty aroma, toss in the whole baby aubergines, coating them in the onion and spices. Tip in the tomatoes, cover with a lid and cook gently for about 40 minutes, until the aubergines are beautifully tender.

Season to taste with salt and pepper and add half the mint and coriander leaves. Cover and simmer for a further 5–10 minutes. Sprinkle with the remaining mint and coriander leaves and serve hot with couscous or bulghur wheat and a dollop of yoghurt.

1–2 tablespoons olive oil

1 tablespoon unsalted butter

1–2 red onions, halved lengthways and sliced with the grain

3–4 garlic cloves, crushed

1–2 red chillies, deseeded and sliced, or 2–3 dried red chillies, left whole

1–2 teaspoons coriander seeds, roasted and crushed

1–2 teaspoons cumin seeds, roasted and crushed

2 teaspoons sugar

16 baby aubergines, with stalks intact

2 x 400-g tins chopped tomatoes

a bunch of fresh mint leaves, roughly chopped

a bunch of fresh coriander, roughly chopped

sea salt and freshly ground black pepper

serves 4

The authentic flavour of a curry comes from using fresh spices (not ones that have been lurking in your very own kitchen graveyard) and the heady, slightly sour taste of bay leaves. Chicken thigh fillets work better here than breast meat, as they are harder to overcook. Warm chapattis and mango chutney make good accompaniments.

chicken & lentil curry

25 g unsalted butter

2 large onions, thinly sliced

2 garlic cloves, crushed

1½ tablespoons garam masala

500 g chicken thigh fillets or breast fillets, cut into chunks

300 g passata (sieved tomatoes)

8 bay or curry leaves

100 g red lentils

400 ml chicken stock

sea salt and freshly ground black pepper

fresh coriander leaves, to garnish (optional)

cucumber yoghurt

140-ml pot natural yoghurt

¼ cucumber, cut into ribbons or chopped

serves 4

Melt the butter in a deep frying pan, add the onions and fry, stirring, over medium heat. Once they are sizzling, cover with a lid, reduce the heat and cook for 10–15 minutes, stirring occasionally.

When the onions have softened, add the garlic and garam masala, cook for a further 3–4 minutes until the spices start to release their aroma and the onions are beginning to turn golden. If you are using chicken thighs, add them now and cook for 5–6 minutes. Add the passata, bay leaves, lentils and stock. If you are using chicken breast, add it now. Cover with a lid and simmer for 15 minutes until the lentils are tender.

To make the cucumber yoghurt, put the yoghurt in a small dish, add a good pinch of salt and stir in the cucumber.

When the curry is cooked, season generously with salt and pepper (lentils tend to absorb a lot of seasoning, so don't be stingy). Transfer to bowls, scatter with coriander, if using, and add a dollop of the cucumber yoghurt. Serve with mango chutney and warm chapattis, rolled up, if desired.

Thai curry is a great flavour hit at the end of a busy day. Ready-made pastes make everything easier, but your curry will only be as good as your paste. Look for Thai brands, which are good but often very hot, or make your own and freeze it in small portions. Serve with steamed jasmine rice.

red curry with prawns & pumpkin

If you remember, put the coconut milk in the fridge as soon as you buy it.

When you are ready to start cooking, scrape off the thick coconut cream that usually clings to the lid and put just the cream in a wok or large saucepan over medium heat. Add the curry paste and stir for 1–2 minutes until the paste smells fragrant, then add the sugar and cook for a further 2 minutes until sticky.

Pour in the rest of the coconut milk, add the lemongrass, pumpkin and 100–120 ml water to almost cover the pumpkin. Bring the contents of the wok to a gentle simmer and leave to bubble away gently for 10 minutes, or until the pumpkin is tender.

Add the sugar snap peas and cook for 2 minutes, then add the prawns and cook for a further 2 minutes or until they turn pink. Remove from the heat and stir in the fish sauce. Transfer to bowls and sprinkle with the mint and chilli. Taste and add more fish sauce if necessary. Serve with steamed jasmine rice.

400-ml tin coconut milk

2 tablespoons red curry paste

2 tablespoons palm sugar or demerara sugar

1 lemongrass stalk, cut in half and bruised

400 g pumpkin or butternut squash, peeled, deseeded and cut into 2-cm chunks

125 g sugar snap peas, cut diagonally

200 g uncooked tiger prawns, shelled, deveined and butterflied but tails intact

2 tablespoons Thai fish sauce

15 fresh mint leaves, finely shredded

1 large red chilli, deseeded and cut into thin strips

serves 4

This fiery curry from southern India is not for the faint-hearted, although you can decrease the amounts of chilli and curry powder to suit your palate. Serve with pickles as well as steamed basmati rice, if you like.

beef madras

To make the marinade, combine the yoghurt and curry powder in a non-metallic bowl. Stir in the beef, season with salt, cover and marinate in the fridge for 24 hours.

Heat the oil in a large non-stick wok or frying pan and add the bay leaf, cinnamon, cloves and cardamom pods. Stir-fry for 1 minute, then add the onion. Stir-fry over medium heat for 4–5 minutes, then add the garlic, ginger, turmeric, red chilli, chilli powder and cumin. Add the marinated beef (discarding the marinade) and stir-fry for 10–15 minutes over low heat.

Pour in the tomatoes and coconut milk and bring to the boil. Reduce the heat to low, cover tightly and simmer gently for 1 hour, stirring occasionally. Stir in the garam masala 5 minutes before the end of cooking.

Check the seasoning. Drizzle with extra coconut milk and garnish with the coriander. Serve immediately with steamed basmati rice and pickles, if you like.

800 g stewing beef, cut into large bite-sized pieces

2 tablespoons sunflower oil

1 dried bay leaf

1 cinnamon stick

3 cloves

4 cardamom pods, bruised

1 large onion, thinly sliced

3 garlic cloves, crushed

1 teaspoon finely grated fresh ginger

1 teaspoon ground turmeric

1 red chilli, split in half lengthways

2 teaspoons hot chilli powder

2 teaspoons ground cumin

200 g tinned chopped tomatoes

300 ml coconut milk, plus extra to drizzle

¼ teaspoon garam masala

sea salt

a small handful of freshly chopped coriander leaves, to garnish

marinade

5 tablespoons natural yoghurt

3 tablespoons Madras curry powder

serves 4

This lightly spiced curry is the perfect comfort food. For the best results, make sure that you use very good-quality organic tinned red kidney beans.

red kidney bean curry

Heat the butter and oil in a large, heavy-based saucepan and add the onion, cinnamon, bay leaves, garlic and ginger and stir-fry for 4–5 minutes. Stir in the turmeric, ground coriander, cumin, garam masala and chillies.

Add the kidney beans, tomato purée and sufficient water to make a thick sauce. Bring to the boil and cook for 4–5 minutes, stirring often.

Season well, drizzle with yoghurt, if desired, and garnish with coriander.

1 tablespoon unsalted butter

2 tablespoons sunflower oil

1 onion, finely chopped

1 cinnamon stick

2 dried bay leaves

3 garlic cloves, crushed

2 teaspoons finely grated fresh ginger

½ teaspoon ground turmeric

1 teaspoon ground coriander

2 teaspoons ground cumin

1 teaspoon garam masala

2 dried red chillies

250 g tinned red kidney beans, drained and rinsed

4 tablespoons tomato purée

sea salt

yoghurt, to drizzle (optional)

freshly chopped coriander leaves, to garnish

serves 4

The vibrant colours of Kerala, India's southern-most state, are all here on a plate. This deliciously creamy curry is made even richer with the addition of that irresistibly moreish snack, the cashew nut. Serve with either steamed or boiled basmati rice.

creamy vegetable curry

2 tablespoons vegetable oil

125 g large, unsalted cashews

6 shallots, peeled and halved

1 teaspoon black mustard seeds

6–8 curry leaves

2 garlic cloves, chopped

1 tablespoon finely grated fresh ginger

1 teaspoon turmeric

4 large dried red chillies

1 small red pepper, thinly sliced

2 ripe tomatoes, quartered

8 very small new potatoes, halved

400-ml tin coconut milk

serves 4

Put the oil in a heavy-based saucepan set over medium heat. Add the cashews and shallots and cook for 5 minutes, stirring often, until the cashews are just starting to brown. Add the mustard seeds and curry leaves and cook until the seeds start to pop. Add the garlic, ginger, turmeric, chillies and red pepper to the pan and stir-fry for 2 minutes, until aromatic.

Add the tomatoes, potatoes and coconut milk, partially cover the pan and leave to simmer gently over low heat for about 20 minutes, or until the potatoes are cooked through. Spoon over basmati rice to serve, if liked.

Aubergines feature in numerous iconic international meat-free dishes, including the spicy Middle Eastern dip baba ghanoush, Sicilian caponata, and the French classic ratatouille. This aubergine curry is tasty as well as colourful. Serve it with basmati rice if you like.

aubergine, tomato & lentil curry

Heat the oil in a frying pan set over high heat. When the oil is smoking hot, add the aubergine and cook for 5 minutes, turning the pieces often so that they cook evenly. At first the aubergine will absorb the oil, but as it cooks to a dark and golden colour, the oil will start to seep out back into the pan. Remove the aubergine from the pan at this point and not before.

Add the onion, garlic and ginger to the pan and cook for 5 minutes. Add the cherry tomatoes and cook for 1 minute, until they just soften and collapse, then remove them from the pan before they break up too much. Set aside with the aubergine.

Add the curry leaves and cumin to the pan and cook for a couple of minutes while the curry leaves pop and crackle. Add the chilli powder, tomato purée, 480 ml water and the lentils. Simmer for 15–20 minutes, until the lentils are tender but retain some 'bite'. Stir in the aubergine and tomatoes and cook the curry for a couple of minutes just to warm through. Stir in the coriander and spoon over boiled or steamed basmati rice to serve, if liked.

3 tablespoons olive oil

1 large aubergine, cut into 8 pieces

1 red onion, chopped

2 garlic cloves, chopped

1 tablespoon finely chopped fresh ginger

250 g cherry tomatoes on the vine

6–8 curry leaves

1 teaspoon ground cumin

¼ teaspoon chilli powder

1 tablespoon tomato purée

125 g red lentils

1 handful of fresh coriander, roughly chopped

serves 4

A mollee is a South Indian sauce, one of those dishes known wrongly in the rest of the world as a curry. It is mostly used for poaching fish, but is also delicious as a medium for reheating cooked meats or vegetables. The first step is to make the sauce: after that, you may add what you like.

fish mollee

500 g firm fish such as salmon, monkfish or cod

1 tablespoon ground turmeric

1 teaspoon sea salt

100 g unsalted butter

1 onion, chopped

1 garlic clove, crushed

2 small fresh green chillies, deseeded if preferred, then chopped

3 cm fresh ginger, peeled and grated

12 cardamom pods, crushed

6 cloves, crushed

1 cinnamon stick

500 ml tinned coconut milk

freshly squeezed lemon juice, to taste

freshly torn coriander leaves, to serve

serves 4

Cut the fish into 3-cm strips. Mix the turmeric and salt on a plate, roll the fish in the mixture and set aside for a few minutes.

Meanwhile, heat the butter in a flameproof casserole or large saucepan. Add the onion, garlic, chillies, ginger, cardamom, cloves and cinnamon stick and fry gently until the onion is softened and translucent.

Add the coconut milk, heat until simmering and cook until the mixture is quite thick. Add the fish to the casserole, then spoon the sauce over the top, making sure the fish is well covered. Cook for 10 minutes, until the fish is opaque all the way through. Serve sprinkled with lemon juice and coriander.

The orange of the butternut squash contrasted with the green of the spinach makes this a particularly colourful dish. Serve with steamed basmati rice and other curry dishes or with naan bread.

spicy butternut & chicken curry

Heat the oil in a non-stick frying pan or wok, add the mustard seeds and fry until they pop. Add half the butternut squash or pumpkin and all of the onions and stir-fry gently until the onions are softened and translucent. Add the garlic, ginger, some salt and pepper and stir-fry for 1 minute. Add the turmeric and stir-fry for 1 minute more.

Add the chicken, stir-fry until sealed on all sides, then add the tomatoes and remaining butternut. Bring to the boil, then reduce the heat and simmer, covered, for about 20 minutes, or until tender.

Add the cream, bring to the boil and simmer, stirring, until thickened – the cream will first boil with large bubbles, then small. Stop at this point or the cream will curdle. Add the spinach and garam masala, cover with a lid and steam for 2 minutes until the leaves collapse, then stir into the rest of the ingredients. Serve with steamed basmati rice and other curry dishes or with naan bread.

2 tablespoons sunflower or groundnut oil

1 tablespoon mustard seeds

500 g butternut squash or pumpkin, peeled, deseeded and cut into 3-cm cubes

2 onions, thinly sliced

2 garlic cloves, crushed

3 cm fresh ginger, peeled and grated (optional)

a pinch of turmeric

4 chicken breasts, skinless and boneless, cut into 2-cm slices

500 g tomatoes, skinned and roughly chopped

250 ml double cream

1 large pack of fresh spinach, about 400 g

a pinch of garam masala

sea salt and freshly ground black pepper

serves 4

bakes & gratins

This absolutely delicious dish, inspired by paella, never fails to impress and delight, and because it's all cooked in the oven, it really couldn't be easier.

oven-roasted spicy macaroni

Preheat the oven to 220°C (400°F) Gas 7.

Put the cherry tomatoes into the roasting tin and sprinkle with the onion, garlic and oil. Roast in the preheated oven for 20 minutes until the tomatoes are soft.

Remove from the oven and add the macaroni, chicken, chorizo, rosemary, stock, saffron, salt and pepper. Mix well and return it to the oven to bake for 30 minutes.

Add the prawns and bake for a further 5 minutes until the pasta and chicken are cooked. Sprinkle with basil and serve.

250 g cherry tomatoes

1 red onion, finely chopped

2 garlic cloves, finely chopped

2 tablespoons olive oil

300 g small macaroni

4 boneless, skinless chicken thighs, quartered crossways

200 g chorizo, thickly sliced

2 teaspoons freshly chopped rosemary

1 litre chicken stock

a pinch of saffron threads

8 large, uncooked prawns

sea salt and freshly ground black pepper

a handful of freshly torn basil, to serve

serves 4

This very versatile dish, served on a base of thyme and lemon, can be prepared in advance. It then needs only to be roasted and basted for an effortless supper. If you wish, you can serve it with a tomato or herb sauce and roast fennel.

roast cod cutlets

6 cod cutlets, 250 g each for a main course, 200 g as a starter

about 30 g unsalted butter

freshly grated nutmeg

6 lemon slices

2 large potatoes, par-boiled in salted water and cut into walnut-sized pieces

sea salt and freshly ground black pepper

base of thyme & lemon

175 g unsalted butter

2 onions, chopped

2 garlic cloves, crushed

1 teaspoon fresh lemon thyme leaves

6 peppercorns

2 bay leaves

serves 6

Preheat the oven to 190°C (375°F) Gas 5.

Season the cutlets with salt and pepper.

To make the base of thyme and lemon, heat the 175 g butter in a frying pan, add the onions, garlic, thyme, peppercorns and bay leaves and cook gently until softened but not browned.

Spread the mixture in a roasting tin. Put the cutlets on top, with about 1 teaspoon of the butter on each piece. Add the nutmeg and lemon slices. Tuck the potato pieces around. Roast in the preheated oven for 35 minutes, basting once with the juices from the lemon slices.

Serve as it is, or with a tomato or herb sauce and roast fennel.

A mixture of very finely chopped vegetables forms the basis of this dish. In can be served either very hot straight from the oven or left until cold, which is delicious in summer. In winter, you could use fresh herrings instead of sardines. Eat it with bread to mop up the juices.

baked sardines

Preheat the oven to 190°C (375°F) Gas 5.

Heat 3 tablespoons of the oil in a frying pan, add the red pepper, onions and garlic and cook gently until softened but not coloured, 8–10 minutes. Add the tomatoes, paprika, saffron, cumin and bay leaves and cook for a further 5–8 minutes (add a little water if the mixture sticks to the pan) until completely cooked. Season with salt and pepper and fold in the chopped parsley.

Put the sardine fillets on a plate, skin side down, and sprinkle with a little salt and pepper.

Arrange one-third of the fillets skin side up in an ovenproof dish. Cover with one-third of the cooked mixture. Repeat twice more – when adding the last layer, let the silver sardine skin peek through. Grind over a little more pepper and spoon over the rest of the oil.

Bake in the preheated oven for 15–20 minutes until sizzling. Sprinkle with parsley leaves, then serve.

5 tablespoons extra virgin olive oil

1 red pepper, deseeded and finely chopped

2 medium onions, finely chopped

3 garlic cloves, crushed

2 large tomatoes, skinned, deseeded and cut into 3-cm cubes

1 teaspoon hot paprika

a pinch of saffron

¼ teaspoon ground cumin

2 bay leaves

2 tablespoons freshly chopped flat leaf parsley, plus extra leaves to serve

9–12 fresh sardine fillets (depending on the size of the dish)

sea salt and freshly ground black pepper

serves 4–6

This Middle Eastern dish supposedly got its name because the priest (the imam) found it so delicious that he swooned. Some stories tell that he fainted because he was horrified at the amount of oil used to cook it. This, of course, is the secret of the dish – aubergines must be cooked well, with large quantities of oil.

imam bayildi

4 large aubergines, with long stalks if possible, halved lengthways

200 ml extra virgin olive oil

500 g onions, halved and very thinly sliced

4 garlic cloves, crushed

750 g plum tomatoes, skinned, deseeded and finely chopped

leaves from 15 sprigs of flat leaf parsley

leaves from 12 sprigs of marjoram

2 teaspoons sugar

1 small lemon, thinly sliced

sea salt and freshly ground black pepper

serves 4–8

Preheat the oven to 200°C (400°F) Gas 6.

Cut a line 5 mm in from the edges of the aubergine halves, then score the flesh inside with a criss-cross pattern. Rub plenty of oil all over the aubergines and season with a little salt. Arrange in a single layer in an ovenproof dish. Cook in the preheated oven for about 30 minutes or until the flesh has just softened.

Heat 75 ml of the oil in a heavy-based frying pan, add the onions and garlic, cover with a lid and cook over low heat until soft. Increase the heat and add the tomatoes. Cook until the juices from the tomatoes have reduced a little, then add salt and pepper to taste. Reserve a few parsley leaves for serving, then chop the remainder together with the marjoram. Add to the onion and tomato mixture, then add the sugar.

Scoop some of the central flesh out of the aubergines, leaving a shell around the outside to hold the base in shape. Chop the scooped-out flesh and add to the tomato mixture. Pile the mixture into the aubergine shells and sprinkle with pepper. Arrange the lemon slices on top. Trail more oil generously over the top, then sprinkle with 4 tablespoons of water.

Cover with foil and bake for 30–40 minutes until meltingly soft. Remove the foil about 10 minutes before the end. Serve, sprinkled with any remaining oil and the reserved parsley.

Cream and potatoes, mingling in the heat of the oven, are almost all you'll find in this well-loved dish. Serve on its own, with a mixed green salad, or as a partner for simple roast meat or poultry.

creamy potato gratin

Preheat the oven to 180°C (350°F) Gas 4.

Put the potatoes in a large saucepan with the milk and bay leaf. Bring to the boil, then lower the heat, add a pinch of salt and simmer gently until part-cooked, 5–10 minutes.

Drain the potatoes. When cool enough to handle (but still hot), slice into rounds about 3 mm thick.

Spread the butter in the bottom of a baking dish. Arrange half the potato slices in the dish and sprinkle with salt. Put the remaining potato on top and sprinkle with more salt. Pour in the cream and sprinkle with the grated nutmeg.

Bake in the preheated oven until golden and the cream is almost absorbed, but not completely, about 45 minutes. Serve hot, on its own or with a mixed green salad, or with simple roast meat or poultry.

2 kg waxy salad-style potatoes, cut in half if large

2 litres whole milk

1 fresh bay leaf

30 g unsalted butter

550 ml whipping cream

a pinch of grated nutmeg

sea salt

serves 4–6

This is a hearty hotpot packed with autumnal vegetables and rich with smoky paprika. Butter beans have a distinctive but delicate flavour. Serve with warm crusty bread to dip in the sauce.

smoky hotpot

2 tablespoons olive oil

1 large onion, chopped

2 garlic cloves, chopped

2 teaspoons smoked paprika

1 celery stick, chopped

1 carrot, chopped

2 medium waxy potatoes, cut into 2-cm dice

1 red pepper, chopped

500 ml vegetable stock

100 g tinned butter beans, drained and rinsed

sea salt and freshly ground black pepper

crusty bread, to serve

serves 4

Put the oil in a saucepan set over medium heat. Add the onion and cook for 4–5 minutes until softened. Add the garlic and paprika to the pan and stir-fry for 2 minutes. Add the celery, carrot, potatoes and red pepper and cook for 2 minutes, stirring constantly to coat the vegetables in the flavoured oil.

Add the stock and butter beans and bring to the boil. Reduce the heat and partially cover the pan with a lid. Leave to simmer for 40 minutes, stirring often, until all the vegetables are cooked. Season to taste and serve with crusty bread.

A few chickpeas are all that are needed to turn an unassuming tray of early-autumn roasted vegetables into a great supper. Serve with some spicy couscous to soak up the tasty juices.

roasted vegetables & chickpeas

Preheat the oven to 180°C (350°F) Gas 4.

Put the mushrooms, tomatoes, red and yellow peppers, onion, fennel and garlic in a large roasting tin. Sprinkle the salt evenly over the vegetables and drizzle with the oil. Roast in the preheated oven for 1 hour.

Remove the tin from the oven and turn the vegetables. Add the chickpeas and thyme sprigs. Return the tin to the oven and roast for a further 30 minutes, until the edges of the vegetables are just starting to blacken and char.

To serve, spoon spiced couscous (if using) onto serving plates and top with the roasted vegetables and chickpeas.

12 small mushrooms

2 ripe tomatoes, halved

1 red pepper, cut into strips

1 yellow pepper, cut into strips

1 red onion, cut into wedges

1 small fennel bulb, sliced into thin wedges

1 garlic bulb, broken into cloves but left unpeeled

2 teaspoons sea salt

2 tablespoons olive oil

400-g tin chickpeas, drained and rinsed

2 fresh thyme or rosemary sprigs

serves 4

The Queensland Blue pumpkin is for some the best pumpkin of all. A squashed turban shape, it is very dense and firm, with a beautiful dark blue-green-grey skin and brilliant orange flesh. Don't worry if you can't find this variety – there are many others that will fit the bill. Choose one large pumpkin or several smaller ones.

baked stuffed pumpkin

1 large pumpkin, about 3 kg, or 6 small pumpkins

olive oil, for brushing

filling

1–2 carrots, sliced

2 tablespoons olive oil

4 slices smoked bacon, chopped

1–2 onions, thinly sliced

3 garlic cloves, crushed

3 cm fresh ginger, peeled and finely chopped

leaves from 3–4 sprigs of oregano or thyme, chopped

500 g beef mince

2 teaspoons tomato purée

1–2 fresh red chillies, halved, deseeded and chopped

250 g cooked white rice

leaves from 1 large bunch of fresh flat leaf parsley, chopped

sea salt and freshly ground black pepper

serves 6–8

Preheat the oven to 200°C (400°F) Gas 6.

Using a small, sharp knife, cut a 'plug' out of the top of the pumpkin, including the stalk, if any, and reserve. Scoop out and discard all the seeds and fibres. Brush the inside of the pumpkin with oil.

Par-boil the carrots in boiling salted water until almost cooked. Drain and set aside.

Put the oil in a non-stick frying pan, add the bacon and stir-fry until crispy. Remove with a slotted spoon and drain on kitchen paper.

Add the onions to the pan and fry until softened and translucent. Add the garlic and ginger and stir-fry until the onion is golden. Add the oregano or thyme and the mince and stir-fry until the meat is browned. Stir in the tomato purée and chillies. Add the carrots, bacon and rice and stir-fry until hot – the mixture should be fairly stiff.

Mix in the parsley then use the mixture to stuff the pumpkin – the mixture is already cooked, so it won't expand. Put the lid on top and envelop the bottom of the pumpkin in a 'basin' of foil. Bake in the preheated oven for 45–60 minutes or until the pumpkin is tender. Test with the point of a skewer – the time will depend on the pumpkin variety and its size.

Baking sliced potatoes and mushrooms in layers allows the potatoes to absorb the juices and earthy flavour of the mushrooms. Try to use the darkest mushrooms you can find – they will have the best taste. You can always mix fresh ones with reconstituted dried mushrooms for a more intense flavour.

potato & mushroom gratin

Preheat the oven to 180°C (350°F) Gas 4.

Peel the potatoes and slice thickly, putting them in a bowl of cold water as you go to stop them from browning. Trim the mushrooms and slice thickly. Put half the potatoes in a layer in the bottom of a well-buttered ovenproof dish, sprinkle with oil and cover with half the mushrooms.

Put the breadcrumbs, Parmesan, parsley and some salt and pepper in a bowl and mix well. Spread half this mixture over the mushrooms, then sprinkle with more oil. Cover with a second layer of potatoes, then a layer of the remaining mushrooms. Finally, sprinkle with the rest of the breadcrumb mixture and more oil.

Cover with foil and bake in the preheated oven for 30 minutes. Uncover and cook for a further 30 minutes until the potatoes are tender and the top is golden brown.

1 kg medium potatoes

750 g flavoursome mushrooms such as dark flat cap, chestnut or portobello (or use fresh wild mushrooms)

extra virgin olive oil, for sprinkling

175 g stale (not dry) white breadcrumbs

4 tablespoons freshly grated Parmesan cheese

4 tablespoons freshly chopped flat leaf parsley

sea salt and freshly ground black pepper

serves 4

casseroles & stews

In its native Basque region of Spain, this stew is called marmitako. The name comes from the French word *marmite* – a tall, straight-sided stewpot made from copper, iron or earthenware. The fishermen used to make this stew on board their boats, using tuna from the Bay of Biscay, and mopping up the soupy juices with lots of delicious fried bread.

tuna & potato stew

Halve and deseed the red, yellow and green peppers and cut the flesh into 1-cm chunks.

Heat the oil in a flameproof casserole, add the onion, garlic and peppers and fry over low heat until softened but not coloured, 12–15 minutes. Increase the heat and stir in the tomatoes and their juice. When the mixture starts to thicken, add the paprika, bay leaf, salt and pepper.

Stir in the potatoes and 400 ml boiling water and simmer gently for about 15 minutes until the potatoes are cooked.

Season the pieces of tuna 10 minutes before cooking. Add the tuna to the casserole and after about 30 seconds, when the underside turns pale, turn the pieces over and turn off the heat. Leave for 5 minutes. Sprinkle with parsley. Serve with triangles of fried bread, if you wish.

1 small red pepper

1 small yellow pepper

1 small green pepper

3 tablespoons extra virgin olive oil

1 large onion, finely chopped

2 garlic cloves, finely chopped

5 tomatoes, skinned, deseeded and chopped (reserve any juices)

½ teaspoon sweet paprika

1 bay leaf

500 g potatoes, peeled and cut into 1-cm slices

2 slices of fresh tuna, 500 g each, cut into 12 chunky pieces

2 tablespoons flat leaf parsley leaves, torn

sea salt and freshly ground black pepper

fried bread, cut into triangles, to serve (optional)

serves 4–6

This easy, stress-free recipe makes a fantastic meal. Don't forget to provide a few empty dishes for discarded shells and some bowls of warm water for washing fingers. Serve with plenty of warm crusty bread.

easy fish stew

5 tablespoons olive oil

3 garlic cloves, crushed and chopped

2 onions, chopped

2 leeks, trimmed and sliced

3 celery stalks, sliced

1 fennel bulb, trimmed and sliced

1 tablespoon plain flour

1 bay leaf

a sprig of thyme

a generous pinch of saffron threads

3 x 410 g tins chopped tomatoes

2 litres fish stock

1 kg monkfish tail, cut Into 8 pieces

500 g mussels in shells, scrubbed

8 scallops

8 uncooked prawns, shell on

a bunch of flat leaf parsley, chopped

sea salt and freshly ground black pepper

serves 8

Heat the oil in a large saucepan and add the garlic, onions, leeks, celery and fennel. Cook over low to medium heat for 10 minutes until soft. Sprinkle in the flour and stir well. Add the bay leaf, thyme, saffron, tomatoes, fish stock and salt and pepper to taste. Bring to the boil, then simmer for 25 minutes.

Add the monkfish, mussels, scallops and prawns, cover with a lid and simmer very gently for 6 minutes. Remove from the heat and set aside, with the lid on, for 4 minutes. Add the parsley and serve with warm crusty bread. Take care not to eat the mussels that haven't fully opened.

Chicken with rice is a universal favourite, and it is always a good bet when entertaining large numbers or mixed ages. The inspiration came from paella, though this is baked, so you can put it in the oven and forget about it, almost, until serving time. The dish tastes better if the ingredients aren't packed in too deeply.

chicken, sausage & rice

Preheat the oven to 200°C (400°F) Gas 6.

Tie the bay leaf, thyme and parsley together with kitchen string.

Heat the oil in a large ovenproof pan with a lid. Add the chicken pieces skin side down and cook on high heat until browned, 3–5 minutes. Repeat on the other side. Work in batches if all the pieces will not fit comfortably in the pan. Transfer the browned chicken to a plate and season with salt and pepper.

Add the sausages to the pan and cook until browned. Remove and cut into 3–4 pieces, depending on their size. Remove and set aside.

Add the onion, red pepper and celery and cook on high heat until they begin to brown and smell aromatic, 2–3 minutes. Add the garlic, chilli flakes and some salt and pepper and cook for 1 minute more.

Stir in the rice until all the grains are coated. Add the wine, stock, tomatoes and some salt and mix well. Add the bunch of herbs, the chicken and sausage.

Cover the pan and bake in the preheated oven until the rice is cooked, about 30 minutes. After 20 minutes, add the peas on top and a little bit of water if the liquid has almost completely evaporated. Cook for 10 minutes more. Remove from the oven and set aside, covered, for 10 minutes. Remove the bunch of herbs and fluff up the rice to mix in the peas. Serve hot.

1 bay leaf

a few sprigs of thyme and flat leaf parsley

1 tablespoon extra virgin olive oil

8 chicken thighs, trimmed

6 pure pork sausages

1 onion, chopped

1 red pepper, chopped

2 celery stalks, chopped

3 garlic cloves, finely chopped

¼–½ teaspoon chilli flakes, or more to taste

370 g paella rice, or other short-grained rice

125 ml dry wine, red or white

300 ml fresh unsalted chicken stock

400-g tin chopped tomatoes

200 g green peas, fresh or frozen and thawed

sea salt and freshly ground black pepper

serves 4–6

These little spring leeks are so small that they are easily confused with spring onions. The green tips are soft and, although people might not want to eat them, they do give a more leeky flavour to the dish if left on. The dish could also be made with aromatic spices like paprika and cumin. It works well alongside couscous mixed with pine nuts.

lemony chicken with leeks

60 g plain flour

1 organic spring chicken, about 1.6 kg, cut into 10 pieces

125 ml olive oil

12 baby leeks

3 garlic cloves, chopped

1 unwaxed lemon, thickly sliced

125 ml white wine

125 ml freshly squeezed lemon juice

125 ml chicken stock

1 tablespoon light soy sauce

sea salt and freshly ground black pepper

serves 4

Season the flour with salt and pepper and put it in a clean plastic bag. Add half the chicken pieces and shake to coat them in the seasoned flour. Repeat with the remaining chicken pieces. Set aside until needed.

Heat the oil in a large frying pan over medium-high heat. Add the leeks and stir-fry for 4 minutes, until softened and silky. Remove the leeks and set aside. Add half of the chicken to the pan and cook in batches for 4–5 minutes, turning each piece often, until golden brown all over. Transfer the browned chicken to a plate and repeat to cook the remaining chicken.

Pour off all but 1 tablespoon of oil from the pan, leaving any sediment in the pan. Add the garlic and lemon and cook for 1 minute, stirring well to combine with any of the cooked-on bits from the bottom of the pan. Add the wine and leave to sizzle for 1 minute, then add the lemon juice, chicken stock and soy sauce and bring to the boil. Return the chicken to the pan and cook for 20 minutes. Turn each piece of chicken, then put the leeks on top of the chicken. Cover the pan with foil and cook for a further 20 minutes, until the chicken is cooked through. Stir to combine the chicken and any of the cooking juices evenly with the leeks. Serve with couscous, if you wish.

The red rice from the Camargue area of southern France used in this dish is justly famous. It takes over twice the usual time to cook but is good served with hearty wine and other intense tastes, as in this easy chicken dish.

camargue chicken

Pat the chicken breasts dry with kitchen paper and cut 2 slashes on top of each.

Heat half the butter and all the oil in a large flameproof casserole and brown the chicken, skin side first, until golden. Remove from the pan and set aside.

Add the garlic and rice to the pan and stir over high heat for 1 minute. Pour in the chicken stock and 300 ml boiling water. Add the white part of the leeks and some salt and pepper. Cover the pan and cook over low heat for 3 minutes. Uncover, then add the chicken pieces, pushing them into the rice. Add the white wine and put the bacon on top.

Increase the heat slightly. Cover the pan again and cook for a further 10 minutes, then add the tarragon vinegar, the fresh tarragon, if using, and the green part of the leeks. Cook for a final 5 minutes, uncover the pan and add the remaining butter, tilting the pan to mix. Serve hot with the same wine used in cooking.

* If red rice is unavailable, you could substitute wild rice, but presoak it for 2 hours in hot (not boiling) water to shorten the cooking time. Drain, then proceed as above.

4 boneless chicken breasts, preferably free range, or 4 chicken quarters

25 g salted butter

4 tablespoons virgin olive oil

2 garlic cloves, chopped

250 g Camargue red rice *

500 ml hot chicken stock

3 leeks, white parts sliced into 5-cm chunks, green tops finely sliced

125 ml robust white wine

6 slices rindless smoked bacon or pancetta, whole or cut into strips

2 tablespoons tarragon vinegar

30–40 fresh tarragon leaves (optional)

sea salt and freshly ground black pepper

serves 4

This is one of the easiest supper dishes imaginable. It takes less time to cook than a ready meal and is much more delicious. You can use any dry white wine, but Viognier, an exotic, slightly scented grape variety, is particularly good. Unoaked or lightly oaked Chardonnay will also work well. Steamed asparagus tips are a good accompaniment.

chicken with white wine

1 tablespoon olive oil

100 g pancetta cubes or dry-cured streaky bacon, chopped

2 skinless, boneless chicken breasts, cut into thin slices

1 small onion, very finely chopped

125 ml full-bodied dry white wine, such as Viognier

150 g green peas, fresh or frozen and thawed

2 tablespoons finely chopped fresh tarragon leaves

100 g crème fraîche

freshly ground black pepper

serves 2

Heat the oil in a large frying pan, then add the pancetta cubes or bacon. Fry for a couple of minutes until the fat starts to run. Add the chicken slices and fry, stirring occasionally, until lightly golden, 4–5 minutes.

Add the onion to the pan and fry for 1–2 minutes. Add the wine and peas and cook until the wine has reduced by about two-thirds. Reduce the heat and stir in the tarragon, crème fraîche and pepper, to taste. Heat gently until almost bubbling.

Remove the pan from the heat. Transfer the chicken to warm plates, spoon over the sauce and serve immediately with steamed asparagus tips, if you wish.

Typically, this traditional French dish is thickened and enriched with butter but here extra virgin olive oil has been used instead. Good-quality red wine vinegar is essential. Cheap vinegar is far too astringent for this dish and will produce a harsh and unpleasant sauce – a far cry from the mouth-watering result you should get.

poulet sauté au vinaigre

Heat 3 tablespoons of the oil in a large frying pan. Season the chicken all over and cook for 3–4 minutes on each side, or until golden. Add the tomatoes and garlic to the pan. Cook for 10–15 minutes, squashing the tomatoes down with the back of a spoon, until they are thick and sticky and have lost all their moisture.

Pour in the red wine vinegar and leave it to bubble for 10–15 minutes, until the liquid has almost evaporated. Pour in the stock, and cook for a further 15 minutes or so, until reduced by half.

Stir in the remaining oil and parsley and serve with salad leaves.

90 ml extra virgin olive oil

a 2-kg chicken, cut into 8 pieces

500 g very ripe cherry tomatoes (or substitute a 400-g tin cherry tomatoes in juice and rinse before using)

2 garlic cloves, crushed

200 ml good-quality red wine vinegar

300 ml chicken stock

a small bunch of flat leaf parsley, chopped

sea salt and freshly ground black pepper

salad leaves, to serve

serves 4–6

The lardons add a special intensity to the flavour of this easy-to-make recipe. Serve with some wild rice on the side to mop up the lovely sauce.

chicken & bacon pot

1 tablespoon olive oil

300 g lardons

250 g button mushrooms

4 chicken breasts

1 garlic clove, crushed

2 shallots, diced

50 g plain flour

500 ml chicken stock

200 ml white wine

1 bay leaf

a handful of fresh flat leaf parsley, chopped

sea salt and freshly ground black pepper

serves 4

Preheat the oven to 180°C (350°F) Gas 4.

Heat the oil in a casserole, add the lardons and mushrooms and cook over medium heat until golden. Transfer to a plate.

Put the chicken breasts in the casserole and quickly brown on both sides. Set aside with the lardons.

Gently fry the garlic and shallots over low heat in the same dish for 5 minutes. Add the flour and mix well. Remove the dish from the heat, slowly pour in the stock and wine, and stir until smooth. Return to the heat and bring to the boil, stirring constantly. Mix in the lardons and mushrooms, then add the chicken breasts, bay leaf and seasoning. Cover and cook in the oven for 30 minutes. Add the parsley just before serving with an accompaniment of wild rice.

Moroccan cuisine often marries sweet and savoury ingredients to surprisingly good effect, as in this richly flavoured sauce. Serve with either bulghur wheat or couscous mixed with parsley and lemon zest and juice.

moroccan honey & lemon chicken

Lightly season the chicken breasts, then heat 1 tablespoon of the honey in a non-stick frying pan. Add the chicken and the garlic and gently fry the chicken breasts for 1 minute on each side over medium heat until caramelized, but watch carefully to ensure that the honey doesn't burn.

Stir the tomatoes into the pan and add the remaining honey, the cinnamon, lemon zest and juice. Bring to a simmer and cook, uncovered, for 15 minutes.

Scatter the toasted almonds over the chicken and sauce. Serve with bulghur wheat or couscous.

4 skinless, boneless chicken breasts, about 130 g each

3 tablespoons clear honey

2 garlic cloves, sliced

400-g tin chopped tomatoes

½ teaspoon ground cinnamon

grated zest and freshly squeezed juice of ½ unwaxed lemon

sea salt and freshly ground black pepper

20 g toasted flaked almonds, to garnish

serves 4

Comfort food at its best, this chicken and barley dish is quick and easy to make, as well as a joy to eat. Choose a selection of your favourite vegetables to serve on the side – baby carrots sprinkled with fresh tarragon make a colourful accompaniment.

chicken & barley supper

2 tablespoons wholemeal flour

500 g skinless, boneless chicken breasts, cut into cubes

100 g lean bacon slices, cut into strips

2 medium onions, chopped

2 carrots, sliced

2 celery sticks, chopped

750–900 ml white wine or chicken stock

3 tablespoons pearl barley, rinsed

1 tablespoon mixed freshly chopped herbs, such as parsley, rosemary, basil and thyme

freshly ground black pepper

freshly chopped flat leaf parsley, to serve

serves 4

Season the flour with pepper, then toss the chicken cubes in the flour. Heat a large non-stick frying pan or saucepan, add the bacon and dry-fry for 5 minutes, stirring frequently, until the fat starts to run. Add the chicken and fry gently for 5–8 minutes, turning frequently, until the chicken is sealed all over. Remove the chicken and bacon from the pan with a slotted spoon and set aside.

Add the onion, carrots, celery and 4 tablespoons of the wine or stock to the pan and gently fry for 5 minutes, until the vegetables are softened. Add the pearl barley, herbs and 600 ml of the wine or stock. Bring to the boil, then cover, reduce the heat and simmer for 1 hour. Add more wine or stock as it is absorbed.

Return the chicken and bacon to the pan and continue to simmer for a further 30 minutes, or until the pearl barley and chicken are tender. Stir occasionally during cooking, adding a little more wine or stock, if necessary. Serve, sprinkled with chopped parsley and accompanied by a selection of your favourite vegetables.

A huge, colourful stew is very festive and inviting, and this one, based on a traditional Portuguese recipe, makes a nice change from the standard repertoire. For best results, use imported Portuguese piri piri sauce. But beware if you've never tried it before – piri piri is very hot, and the heat varies from one brand to another. Serve with couscous.

lamb stew with piri piri

Preheat the oven to 190°C (375°F) Gas 5.

To make the marinade, put the onion, vinegar, paprika, garlic, coriander, parsley and salt in a large non-metallic dish. Mix well. Add the lamb and turn to coat thoroughly. Cover with clingfilm and refrigerate for at least 3 hours or overnight.

Heat the oil in a large ovenproof saucepan with a lid. When hot, add the lamb and all the marinade. Sprinkle with the flour and stir to coat well. Cook to sear the meat, 3–5 minutes, then stir in 250 ml water. Add the potatoes, carrots, some salt and piri piri and mix well. Cover and transfer to the preheated oven for 50 minutes.

Add the courgettes and red pepper and continue cooking for another 40 minutes. Remove from the oven and stir in the chickpeas. Add salt and pepper to taste, and more piri piri if you like. Serve hot, with couscous on the side.

1 kg boneless lamb, cubed

2 tablespoons extra virgin olive oil

1½ tablespoons flour

500 g potatoes, peeled and cut into large chunks

500 g carrots, cut into large pieces

1–2 teaspoons piri piri sauce

750 g courgettes, cut into thick rounds

1 red pepper, deseeded and cut into pieces

400-g tin unsalted chickpeas, drained and rinsed

sea salt and freshly ground black pepper

marinade

1 onion, chopped

6 tablespoons sherry vinegar

1½ teaspoons sweet smoked paprika

4 garlic cloves, sliced

a large handful of fresh coriander, chopped

a large handful of fresh flat leaf parsley, chopped

1 tablespoon sea salt

serves 6

Herald in the spring with this lamb stew with vegetables instead of a traditional Sunday roast – it's filling and much less effort to make. Serve with boiled baby new potatoes.

spring lamb stew

1 tablespoon sunflower oil

700 g lamb neck fillet, cubed

500 g lamb chump chops, each one cut into several pieces

1 tablespoon plain flour

2 ripe tomatoes, skinned, deseeded and chopped

2 garlic cloves, crushed

600 ml fresh lamb or chicken stock

1 fresh bay leaf

a sprig of thyme

4 baby carrots, cut into 3-cm pieces

200 g baby leeks, cut into 5-cm lengths

200 g baby turnips

200 g sugar snap peas

a handful of fresh flat leaf parsley, chopped

sea salt and freshly ground black pepper

serves 4

Heat the oil in a large casserole, add the lamb and brown the pieces on all sides, in batches if necessary. When all the lamb has been browned, return it all to the pan, lower the heat slightly and stir in a pinch of salt and the flour. Cook, stirring to coat evenly, for 1 minute.

Add the tomatoes and garlic. Stir in the stock, bay leaf and thyme. Bring to the boil and skim off any foam that rises to the surface. Reduce the heat, then cover and simmer gently for 40 minutes.

Add the carrots, leeks and turnips and cook for 25 minutes more. Taste and adjust the seasoning with salt and pepper.

Add the peas and cook for 7 minutes. Sprinkle with the parsley and serve immediately.

A fantastic dish that can be made in advance and finished off on the day: this makes your life easier and also improves the flavour of the dish. All the vegetables can be altered to suit your taste: try leeks, cauliflower and broccoli florets, asparagus, parsnips, turnips, pumpkin or sweet potatoes – the list is endless. Serve with garlic bread.

lamb navarin

Trim any excess fat from the lamb. Heat the oil in a large flameproof casserole or saucepan, add the lamb and cook briefly until browned all over. Depending on the size of the pan, you may have to do this in batches.

Return all the meat to the pan, sprinkle with a fine dusting of flour, mix well and repeat until all the flour has been incorporated. Add the stock, tomatoes, tomato purée, wine, herbs, paprika, garlic and shallots. Mix well and bring to the boil. Reduce the heat and simmer gently for 1 hour, stirring from time to time. Add salt and pepper to taste. (If making in advance, prepare up to this point, leave to cool, then chill overnight.)

Add the carrots, potatoes and celery and cook for 15 minutes. Add the runner beans and curly kale or greens and stir gently. Cover with a lid and cook for a further 5 minutes. Serve with garlic bread.

2 kg boneless leg or shoulder of lamb, cubed

3 tablespoons olive oil

3 tablespoons plain flour

1 litre vegetable stock

2 x 400-g tins chopped tomatoes

1 tablespoon tomato purée

150 ml red wine

2 bay leaves

2 sprigs of marjoram

½ teaspoon smoked paprika

2 garlic cloves, crushed and chopped

8 shallots, finely chopped

300 g baby carrots

300 g new potatoes

3 celery sticks, cut into chunks

100 g runner beans, chopped

50 g curly kale or other greens, coarsely chopped

sea salt and freshly ground black pepper

serves 8

This Greek-style dish is very simple but surprisingly effective, considering how few ingredients there are, so make sure you adjust the seasoning carefully, as it makes such a difference. Trim the stem end only of the okra, to discourage the sticky liquid from oozing out. Serve with new potatoes sprinkled with freshly chopped parsley.

braised lamb with okra

3 tablespoons olive oil

4 lamb steaks, about 1 kg, cut from the leg and deboned

1 small onion, sliced

2 garlic cloves, crushed

4 tomatoes, skinned and deseeded

250 g okra, trimmed

sea salt and freshly ground black pepper

serves 4

Preheat the oven to 180°C (350°F) Gas 4.

Heat the oil in a large, shallow, flameproof casserole or saucepan. Season the meat with salt and pepper, add to the pan and brown the pieces all over. Remove the meat with a slotted spoon, put on a plate and set aside in a warm place.

Add the onion and garlic to the pan and cook until softened and lightly browned. Add the tomatoes and simmer to a pulp.

Return the lamb to the pan, turn to coat, taste and adjust the seasoning and cover with a lid. Bring to the boil on top of the stove, then transfer to the preheated oven and simmer for 20 minutes.

Add the okra, cover and simmer for a further 20 minutes, removing the lid for the last 10 minutes of cooking time, to let the liquid reduce enough to just coat the meat without becoming oily. Serve with new potatoes, sprinkled with freshly chopped parsley.

This version of a daube, a classic French dish made with beef and red wine, contains walnut halves and Cognac – heart-warming, welcoming and grand. Use good quality extra virgin olive oil. Serve hot – either on its own, or with accompaniments such as pasta, mashed potatoes or rice.

boeuf en daube

Cut the beef into 6-cm squares. Heat the oil in a large flameproof casserole and gently fry the garlic, bacon, carrots and onions for about 4–5 minutes or until aromatic. Remove from the casserole. Put a layer of meat in the bottom of the casserole, then add half the fried vegetable mixture and a second layer of meat. Add the remaining vegetable mixture, the tomatoes, orange zest, herbs and walnuts.

Put the wine into a small saucepan and bring to the boil. Add the Cognac or brandy and warm for a few seconds, shaking the pan a little, to let the alcohol cook away. Season the sauce to taste with salt and pepper. Pour the hot liquids over the meat with just enough stock so that it's barely covered.

Heat the casserole until simmering, then cover with foil and a lid and simmer gently for 2 hours or until the meat is fork-tender and the juices rich and sticky.

Sprinkle with the parsley. Serve the casserole on its own, or with pasta, mashed potatoes or rice.

1 kg beef, such as shoulder or topside, cut into 1-cm thick slices

4 tablespoons extra virgin olive oil

4 garlic cloves, sliced

125 g thick-cut unsmoked bacon, cut into small dice

3 carrots, halved lengthways

12–16 baby onions, peeled

6 plum tomatoes, skinned, then thickly sliced

zest of 1 orange, removed in one piece

1 bunch of fresh herbs, such as parsley, thyme, bay leaf and rosemary, tied with kitchen string

60 g walnut halves

250 ml robust red wine

2 tablespoons Cognac or brandy

150 ml beef stock or water

sea salt and freshly ground black pepper

freshly chopped flat leaf parsley, to serve

serves 4–6

To many connoisseurs, brisket is the cut that gives the true, full flavour of beef. No nonsense about having it rare or medium or whatever – this is always well done (and slowly). The meat may be cooked for even longer at the low temperature without any loss of flavour or texture, and some people say the longer, the better. Keep basting and stirring.

brisket & vegetables

1.5 kg beef brisket, boned but not rolled

4 onions, cut into chunks

4 carrots, cut into chunks

4 celery sticks, cut into 5-cm slices

your choice of other vegetables, such as parsnips, leeks and celeriac

4 medium potatoes, par-boiled and quartered

sea salt and freshly ground black pepper

serves 4–6

Season the meat with salt and pepper and put in a large roasting tin.

Put the tin in a cold oven and turn the temperature to 250°C (500°F) Gas 9 for the first 40 minutes. This will start the fat running. Add the onions, carrots, celery and your choice of other vegetables – but not the potatoes. Stir them around to coat with the fat and season lightly with salt and pepper. Reduce the oven temperature to 170°C (325°F) Gas 3.

After another 40 minutes, pour in 500 ml hot water, baste the meat and stir the vegetables with a wooden spoon. Repeat after a further 40 minutes, judging the quantity of water to be added. There should be enough for basting, but the meat should not be awash with liquid. Add the potatoes.

Baste again after another 40 minutes, this time without adding water, and then increase the temperature to 220°C (425°F) Gas 7 for the last 20 minutes.

Remove the roasting tin from the oven and transfer the meat to a large plate. Keep it warm. Pour off all the liquid from the roasting tin through a fine sieve into a jug, leaving most of the fat behind.

Dish up the meat onto a large serving platter with the vegetables around it. Serve the jug of gravy separately.

Inspired by thrift, this dish has transcended its humble origins and become a firm favourite around the world. The golden potato topping hides tender lamb in heavenly gravy.

lancashire hotpot

Preheat the oven to 180°C (350°F) Gas 4.

Heat the oil in a large, flameproof casserole, add the lamb and brown all over. Transfer to a plate. Reduce the heat under the casserole, add all the vegetables, then gently fry for 10 minutes, stirring frequently.

Remove the casserole from the heat, add the meat, then sprinkle in the flour and mix well. Pour in just enough hot water to cover the meat and vegetables, stir well and return to the heat.

Bring the casserole to the boil, stirring frequently as the gravy thickens. Season and add the Worcestershire sauce. Remove from the heat.

Slice the potatoes thinly by hand or with a mandolin. Layer them carefully over the meat and vegetables, covering them completely. Place in the oven and cook for 2 hours. The potatoes should be golden on top and the gravy bubbling up around the sides.

2 tablespoons olive oil

800 g lamb neck fillet, cut into 5-cm pieces

1 onion, finely diced

2 carrots, finely diced

4 celery sticks, finely diced

2 leeks, thinly sliced

2 tablespoons plain flour

1 tablespoon Worcestershire sauce

800 g potatoes, unpeeled

sea salt and freshly ground black pepper

serves 4–6

Think of chilly, dark evenings and this dish is exactly what you would want to eat. The feather-light cheesy dumplings nestling in the rich, savoury casserole will have everyone hungry for more.

beef & carrot casserole

1 tablespoon olive oil

2 garlic cloves, crushed

1 onion, diced

2 celery sticks, diced

800 g chuck steak, cut into cubes

400 ml beef stock

200 ml red wine

2 bay leaves

25 g plain flour

4 carrots, cut into small chunks

sea salt and freshly ground black pepper

dumplings

200 g plain flour

1 teaspoon baking powder

75 g vegetable shortening

75 g strong Cheddar cheese, grated

serves 4–6

Heat the oil in a large casserole, add the garlic, onion and celery and gently fry for 4 minutes. Transfer to a plate. Put the beef in the casserole, increase the heat and gently fry for 5 minutes, stirring frequently. When the beef is cooked, return the onion mixture to the casserole. Add the stock, red wine, bay leaves and seasoning, bring to the boil, then reduce the heat to a gentle simmer. Cover and cook for 1½ hours.

To make the dumplings, place the flour and baking powder in a bowl and rub in the fat until it resembles breadcrumbs. Add the cheese, mixing it in with a knife. Add 75–100 ml water and use your hands to bring the mixture together and form a dough. Divide into 8 equal pieces and roll into balls.

Remove the casserole from the heat for 5 minutes, then sift in the flour and stir to thicken the gravy. Return to the heat, add the carrots and stir until the casserole comes to a simmer. Place the dumplings on top, cover and cook for 20 minutes.

Simple dishes are often the best, and they don't come much simpler than this. Long, slow cooking is the secret of the bolognese sauce, which forms the base of the recipe. You can add more or less cayenne pepper, depending on how hot you like your food. Serve with either bread or boiled rice and a bowl of guacamole.

chilli con carne

Heat the oil in a large saucepan, add the garlic, onions, celery and carrot and fry gently for 10 minutes. Add the beef, breaking it up with a wooden spoon, and cook for a further 10 minutes. Add the oregano, thyme, bay leaves, tomato purée, passata, cayenne, paprika, wine and beans. Season and mix well. Simmer for 1 hour, stirring frequently.

Just before serving, stir in the coriander. Serve with bread or boiled rice and guacamole.

2 tablespoons olive oil

3 garlic cloves, crushed

2 onions, diced

1 celery stick, diced

1 carrot, diced

700 g minced beef

a handful of oregano, chopped

a sprig of thyme

2 bay leaves

2 tablespoons tomato purée

1 litre tomato passata (sieved tomatoes)

1 tablespoon cayenne pepper

1 tablespoon paprika

1 glass of red wine

2 x 400-g tins red kidney beans, drained and rinsed

a handful of coriander, chopped

serves 4–6

The inclusion of fish sauce and spices in this beef casserole gives it an unusual Vietnamese flavour. A crusty baguette is an ideal accompaniment for mopping up the juices.

Vietnamese-style beef

1 stalk of lemongrass, peeled and finely chopped

leaves from 3 sprigs of mint, chopped

2 tablespoons fish sauce

1 teaspoon brown sugar

3 cm fresh ginger, peeled and grated

1 red chilli, deseeded and chopped

2 garlic cloves, crushed

1 kg boneless beef (shin or chuck), cut into 3-cm cubes

2 tablespoons groundnut oil

2 tablespoons tomato purée

3 tomatoes, skinned, deseeded and chopped, about 500 g

freshly ground black pepper

6 spring onions, shredded, to serve

sprigs of mint, to serve

serves 4–6

Put the lemongrass, mint, fish sauce, sugar, ginger, chilli, garlic and lots of freshly ground black pepper in a bowl and mix well.

Add the beef and turn to coat. Cover and marinate in the refrigerator for about 2 hours or overnight.

Heat the oil in a casserole, then add the beef in batches and fry until browned on all sides. Using a slotted spoon, remove each batch to a plate and keep it warm while you cook the remainder.

Return all the beef to the pan, add the tomato purée and tomatoes and cook for 3–4 minutes until they start to break down. Add 1 litre water and bring to the boil. Reduce the heat and simmer for about 2 hours until the meat is spoon-tender and the sauce rich but not too thick.

Serve in small bowls, topped with shredded spring onions and mint sprigs, accompanied by a crusty baguette.

Taking its name from Brunswick County in Virginia, this is a dish designed for a large number of hungry people: it's not sophisticated, just full of goodness. Traditionally, the stew was thickened with mashed potatoes but, in this modern version, they are served separately. Apparently, squirrel used to be one of the ingredients!

brunswick stew

Put the chicken, ham bone or gammon, beef and bay leaf into a large stockpot or casserole and cover with the stock or water. Do not season unless the gammon is unsalted. Cover with a lid, bring to the boil, then reduce the heat and simmer for about 40 minutes.

Lift out the chicken pieces and ham bone or gammon and transfer to a large plate. Leave to cool and then cut off their meat in chunks and set aside. Discard the bones.

Continue simmering until the beef comes away from the centre bone, about 2–4 hours. Discard the bone and add the beef to the chicken and gammon.

If necessary, reduce the pan juices to about 850 ml by boiling hard, then add the onion, tomatoes, celery, broad beans, basil and parsley. Cover and simmer for about 20 minutes until done.

Return the meats to the casserole. If using corn, strip the kernels from the cob and add them to the casserole. Add the chilli and some pepper, simmer for 5 minutes, taste and adjust the seasoning. Serve with piles of buttery mashed potatoes.

1 kg chicken, cut into 4, or 4 leg portions

1 ham bone or uncooked smoked gammon

750 g shin bone beef or osso buco

1 bay leaf

1.75 litres ham stock or water

1 onion, sliced

500 g tomatoes, halved, deseeded and chopped

250 g celery, chopped

250 g broad beans

1½ tablespoons fresh basil, chopped

1½ tablespoons freshly flat leaf parsley, chopped

1 ear of fresh corn (optional)

1 red serrano chilli, deseeded and sliced

sea salt and freshly ground black pepper

serves 8–10

A 'hand' of pork is part of the shoulder of the animal. It is ideal for roasting or braising, as it has just the right amount of fat. A certain amount of fat is needed in this dish to moisten the beans – or perhaps it's the other way round and the beans are needed to mop up the juices. Either way, it makes for a scrumptious dinner.

pork & bean casserole

4 tablespoons olive oil

350 g carrots, cut into 3-cm chunks

4 onions, peeled but left whole

4 small turnips

1 sprig of thyme

1 bay leaf

6 peppercorns

6 garlic cloves, chopped

2 kg hand of pork

250 g rindless smoked streaky bacon in one piece, cut into chunks

250 g tinned cannellini beans, drained and rinsed

750 g small potatoes, peeled

250 g fresh green beans

sea salt and freshly ground black pepper

serves 4

Preheat the oven to 170°C (325°F) Gas 3.

Heat the oil in a large ovenproof casserole with a lid, then stir in the carrots, onions, turnips, thyme, bay leaf, peppercorns and garlic. Gently fry until softened but not browned.

Meanwhile, cut the rind off the pork and reserve it. Add the pork, its rind, the bacon chunks and cannellini beans to the casserole. Cover with water, add salt and pepper and bring to the boil on top of the stove. Transfer to the preheated oven and simmer for 1½ hours, or until the beans are tender.

After 1 hour, taste and adjust the seasoning, then add the potatoes for the last 30 minutes and the fresh green beans for the last 5 minutes.

To serve, remove and discard the pork rind, lift the meat onto a dish and carve into thick slices. Add the vegetables and beans to the dish and serve with a separate small jug of the cooking juices.

There are few ingredients in this dish, so the tomatoes must be of premium quality and vine-ripened in the summer sun. Serve with crusty bread for dipping into the rich sauce.

mediterranean lentil stew

Put the lentils in a large saucepan, add sufficient cold water to cover and set over high heat. Bring to the boil, then reduce the heat and leave to simmer for 20 minutes until the lentils are tender but retain a little 'bite'. Drain and set aside until needed.

Put the oil in a saucepan set over high heat. Add the onion, garlic, oregano and chilli flakes and cook for 5 minutes, stirring often, until the onion softens. Add the capers, tomatoes, passata, lentils and 250 ml water. Bring to the boil, then reduce the heat and leave to simmer gently for 10 minutes, stirring occasionally.

Spoon into warmed serving dishes, top with the olives and crumbled feta and serve with crusty bread on the side for dipping into the sauce.

100 g green or brown lentils

3 tablespoons olive oil

1 onion, chopped

2 garlic cloves, chopped

a small handful of fresh oregano, chopped

1 teaspoon dried chilli flakes

1½ tablespoons salted capers, rinsed

2 ripe tomatoes, roughly chopped

250 ml passata (sieved tomatoes)

60 g small black olives, to serve

100 g feta cheese, crumbled, to serve

serves 4

In Jamaica, callaloo leaves and yam would be used to make this spicy vegetable stew instead of spinach and sweet potato. A plantain is a large cooking banana (some have delightful pale pink flesh), but you can use ordinary green bananas instead.

caribbean vegetable stew

Put the oil in a large, flameproof casserole, add the white onion and cook until softened and translucent. Add the allspice, cumin, nutmeg, chillies, garlic, ginger, tomatoes and parsley and cook until you reach the consistency of a sauce. Season with the soy sauce.

Add the sweet potato, red onions and plantains or bananas, cover and simmer for 20 minutes, then add the carrots and spinach and cook for a further 5 minutes, adding the mangetout for the last 2 minutes. Season, scatter with chives, then serve.

4 tablespoons sunflower oil

1 white onion, chopped

2 teaspoon ground allspice

1 teaspoon ground cumin

¼ teaspoon freshly grated nutmeg

4 fresh red chillies, deseeded and chopped

4 garlic cloves, crushed

5 cm fresh ginger, peeled and grated

5 tomatoes, skinned, deseeded and diced

1 tablespoon freshly chopped flat leaf parsley

2 tablespoons soy sauce

1 sweet potato, peeled and cubed

2 red onions, quartered

2 plantains or green bananas, peeled and cut into chunks

6 baby carrots, trimmed

500 g baby spinach

50 g mangetout

freshly ground black pepper

freshly snipped chives, to serve

serves 4

one-pot desserts

Plums have such a rich flavour when they are cooked that they need little or no other flavourings with them, except perhaps a pinch of cinnamon. This is a great favourite with children, especially when made with greeny-red Victoria plums. Try it with greengages, mirabelles or yellow plums – they will all be delicious. For a grown-up crumble, toss the uncooked plums in a little damson or sloe gin.

simple plum crumble

Preheat the oven to 180°C (350°F) Gas 4 and set a baking tray on the middle shelf to heat.

Halve the plums and remove the stones. Cut the halves into quarters if they are very large. Toss them with the sugar and tip them into an ovenproof baking dish.

To make the crumble topping, rub the butter into the flour with the salt until it resembles rough breadcrumbs. Alternatively, do this in a food processor. Stir in the sugar. (At this point the mixture can be popped in a plastic bag and chilled until ready to cook.)

Lightly scatter the topping mixture over the plums. Place the dish on the baking tray in the preheated oven and bake for 40–45 minutes, until golden brown.

Remove from the oven and serve warm with pouring cream.

8–10 ripe plums
4–5 tablespoons sugar

crumble topping
75 g unsalted butter, chilled
175 g plain flour
a pinch of salt
50 g caster sugar
pouring cream, to serve

serves 4–6

The word 'slump' seems to describe perfectly the sloppy batter that covers the seasonal fruit in this satisfying pudding. Any juicy fruit or berries can be used, and you can substitute pine nuts for almonds and sprinkle them all over the batter. You can also add a drop or two of almond essence to the batter for a stronger flavour.

apricot & almond slump

600 g fresh apricots

100 g golden caster sugar

almond slump batter

200 g plain flour

1 tablespoon baking powder

a pinch of salt

50 g golden caster sugar

100 g ground almonds

about 350 ml milk

4 tablespoons unsalted butter, melted

30 g whole blanched almonds

vanilla ice cream, to serve

serves 4–6

Preheat the oven to 190°C (375°F) Gas 5.

Halve the apricots, remove the stones and mix with the sugar. Set aside until needed.

To make the batter, sift together the flour, baking powder and salt and mix with the sugar in a bowl. Stir in the ground almonds, the milk and melted butter and whisk until smooth and thick. Pour the batter into a large, lightly buttered baking tin, then push in the apricots cut side up, but in a higgledy-piggledy manner and slightly at an angle all over. Place a whole almond inside each apricot where the stone once was.

Bake the slump for 25–30 minutes in the middle of the preheated oven, until risen and golden.

Remove from the oven and allow to cool slightly before serving with vanilla ice cream.

Ripe figs need almost nothing done to them – but if you bake them with lots of vanilla and lemon-scented sugar, and hide a walnut in the middle of each one, you will end up with something divine! Take care not to overcook them otherwise they will collapse.

figs baked with vanilla & lemon

Preheat the oven to 230°C (450°F) Gas 8.

Cut a deep cross in the top of each fig so that they open up a little. Push a walnut half into each cross. Pack the figs closely together in a shallow baking dish.

Chop the vanilla pods and put into a food processor. Add the sugar and lemon zest and process until the pods and zest are chopped into tiny bits. Spoon the mixture over each fig and around the dish. Moisten with white wine.

Bake in the preheated oven for 10 minutes until the sugar melts and the figs start to caramelize. Remove from the oven and leave to cool for a few minutes before serving with thick cream. Alternatively, serve cold with ice cream.

12 large ripe figs

12 walnut halves

2 soft, plump vanilla pods

125 g sugar

grated zest from 1 unwaxed lemon

3 tablespoons white wine

thick double cream or ice cream, to serve

serves 6

This is one of the best ways of cooking pears – it is so simple to make, yet tastes very luxurious. Choose pears that are ripe but not too soft, or they will overcook in the oven. If you can't find a good rich Marsala or Vin Santo, use sweet sherry or Madeira instead.

caramelized pears

6 large ripe pears

150 g caster sugar

150 ml Marsala or Vin Santo

200 g mascarpone cheese

1 vanilla pod, split, seeds scraped out and reserved

serves 6

Preheat the oven to 190°C (375°F) Gas 5.

Cut the pears in half and scoop out the cores – do not peel them. Sprinkle the sugar into a flameproof, ovenproof pan or dish. Set over medium heat and let the sugar melt and caramelize. Remove from the heat as soon as it reaches a medium-brown colour and quickly arrange the pears cut side down in the caramel.

Bake in the preheated oven until the pears are soft, for 20–25 minutes. Carefully lift out the pears and set aside, keeping the caramel in the pan.

Put the pan on top of the stove over medium heat and add the Marsala or Vin Santo. Bring to the boil, stirring to dislodge any set caramel, and boil fast until reduced and syrupy. Set aside.

Scoop out a good teaspoon from each cooked pear and put it in a bowl. Add the mascarpone and vanilla seeds and beat well. Fill the centres of the pears with the mascarpone mixture. Return to the oven for 5 minutes until it has heated through. Serve with the caramel sauce spooned over the top.

Using frozen summer berries for this recipe is convenient and also means that you can make it year-round. Serve with crunchy biscuits such as biscotti.

spiced berry compote

Put the frozen berries in a saucepan with the sugar, cinnamon and 2 tablespoons of water. Cover and simmer for 5 minutes or until the berries have defrosted and are juicy.

Blend the arrowroot or cornflour with a little cold water, then mix into the pan. Heat, stirring, until the compote has thickened. Pour into a bowl and leave to cool.

Serve the compote lightly swirled into the yoghurt, with biscotti on the side, if you wish.

325 g frozen summer berries

30 g caster sugar

a pinch of ground cinnamon or 1 cinnamon stick

2 teaspoons arrowroot or cornflour

600 ml Greek yoghurt, to serve

serves 4

This is a pretty marbled dessert of crushed raspberries with a luxurious hint of white chocolate. To make the recipe lighter, you can use low-fat fromage frais.

white chocolate & raspberry fool

40 g white chocolate

125 g fresh raspberries

200 g natural fromage frais

serves 2

Chop the chocolate and put in a heatproof bowl set over a saucepan of gently simmering water until melted. Remove from the heat and leave to cool for a couple of minutes.

Reserve 6 raspberries to decorate, then roughly crush the remaining raspberries with a fork.

Mix the fromage frais into the melted chocolate, then gently fold in the crushed raspberries to give a marbled effect. Spoon into 2 glasses and decorate with the reserved raspberries. Cover and chill in the fridge until ready to serve.

These soft, pear-shaped fruits have a sweet, honey-nectar flavour that is lovely with cured meats and cheese. Once picked, they ripen very quickly, and late-season figs are perfect cooked in puddings.

fig & honey croissant pudding

Preheat the oven to 180°C (350°F) Gas 4.

Put the croissant pieces in the bottom of a lightly greased baking dish. Arrange the fig halves in between the croissant pieces and drizzle the honey over the top.

Combine the eggs, milk, single cream and sugar in a bowl and pour into the dish. Leave to stand for about 20 minutes so that the croissants can absorb some of the custard. Bake in the preheated oven for 50 minutes, until the top of the pudding is a dark golden brown.

Leave to cool a little before cutting into slices and serving with dollops of double cream on the side.

Variation When figs aren't in season, you can lightly spread each piece of croissant with some good-quality fig jam before putting into the dish. Leave out the honey and add 60 g flaked almonds to the egg mixture instead.

2 croissants, preferably stale, each torn into 6 pieces

6 fresh figs, halved

60 ml clear honey

3 eggs

250 ml whole milk

250 ml single cream

55 g caster sugar

double cream, to serve

serves 4

Baked fruit may seem old-fashioned and stodgy, but not these, especially if you use a crisp eating apple. This recipe is sheer heaven and perhaps the easiest cooked pudding you will ever make. Allow one small apple and half a pear per person and serve with plain Greek yoghurt.

baked apples & pears

2 apples, preferably Cox or Braeburn

1 just-ripe pear, preferably Conference

20 g whole hazelnuts, coarsely chopped

6 soft prunes, chopped

4–5 dried figs, chopped

a pinch of ground cinnamon

4 tablespoons unsalted butter

4 teaspoons clear honey

plain Greek yoghurt, to serve

serves 2

Preheat the oven to 200°C (400°F) Gas 6.

Peel the apples. If necessary, trim the bottom slightly so they sit flat. Remove the cores with a small knife or a corer. Using a small spoon, scrape out some apple to make space for more stuffing. Don't go all the way down to the bottom. Peel the pear, halve and scoop out the core, as for the apple.

Put the hazelnuts, prunes and figs in a small bowl and stir well.

Arrange the apples and pears in a baking dish. Stuff the nut mixture into the apple and pear cavities, mounding it at the top. Top each with a light sprinkling of cinnamon, 1 tablespoon butter and trickle over a teaspoon or so of honey. Cover with foil.

Bake in the preheated oven for 20 minutes, then remove the foil and continue baking until just golden, 10–15 minutes more. Divide the apples and pears carefully between the plates and pour over any pan juices. Serve warm, with plain Greek yoghurt.

This American classic is made here with crème fraîche instead of traditional buttermilk. It should be eaten soon after baking as the dough soaks up the fruit juices. Add a punnet of blackberries to the peaches, if you like, or use a combination of peaches, apricots and blackberries.

peach cobbler

Preheat the oven to 190°C (375°F) Gas 5.

Cut the peaches in half, remove the stones, then cut each half into 3 slices. Put them in a shallow baking dish, sprinkle with the flour and toss well to coat evenly. Add the lemon juice and honey and stir. Set aside.

To make the topping, put the cream and crème fraîche in a large bowl and stir well. Set aside.

Put the flour, sugar, baking powder, bicarbonate of soda and salt in a large bowl and mix well. Add the butter and mix with your fingertips until the mixture resembles coarse crumbs. Using a fork, stir in the cream mixture until blended – use your hands at the end if necessary – the mixture should be sticky, thick and not willing to blend easily.

Drop spoonfuls of the mixture on top of the peaches, leaving gaps to expose the fruit. Sprinkle sugar liberally on top of the batter. Bake in the preheated oven until golden, 25–35 minutes. Serve warm with cream or ice cream.

6 peaches, not too ripe

1 tablespoon plain flour

1 tablespoon freshly squeezed lemon juice

3 tablespoons clear honey

cream or vanilla ice cream, to serve

cobbler topping

125 ml double cream

5 tablespoons crème fraîche

165 g plain flour

50 g sugar, plus extra for sprinkling

1 teaspoon baking powder

¼ teaspoon bicarbonate of soda

a pinch of salt

4 tablespoons unsalted butter

2–3 tablespoons sugar, for sprinkling

serves 6

index

recipe credits

Nadia Arumguram
Chicken & yellow
    bean stir-fry
Chinese lemon
    chicken
Five-spice duck
Jasmine rice with
    crab & asparagus
Spiced mixed
    vegetables
Thai-flavour pork
Tofu & mushroom
    noodles

Ghillie Basan
Chicken & olive tagine
Spicy chicken tagine
Summer tagine of
    lamb
Tagine of baby
    aubergines

Fiona Beckett
Chicken with white
    wine

Maxine Clark
Apricot & almond
    slump
Artichoke & pecorino
    risotto
Bacon & eggs in a pan
Caramelized pears
Courgette flower
    risotto
Figs baked with vanilla
    & lemon
Green herb risotto
Potato & mushroom
    gratin
Ratatouille
Saffron potato salad
Simple plum crumble
Wild mushroom
    risotto

Ross Dobson
Aubergine, tomato
    & lentil curry
Creamy vegetable
    curry
Fig & honey croissant
    pudding
Lemony chicken with
    leeks
Mediterranean lentil
    stew
Orange vegetable pilaf
Roasted vegetables
    & chickpeas
Smoky hotpot
Tabbouleh with
    chickpeas
Vegetarian paella

Clare Ferguson
Boeuf en daube
Camargue chicken
Chicken & pork paella
Spanish potato
    omelette

Silvana Franco
Oven-roasted spicy
    macaroni

Liz Franklin
Bang-bang chicken
Italian vegetable
    & bread soup
Marinated mushrooms
Poulet sauté au
    vinaigre

Tonia George
Chicken & lentil curry
Harrira
Lamb & broad bean
    tagine
Lentil, spinach & cumin
    soup
Minestrone
Pad thai
Red curry with prawns
    & pumpkin

Stir-fried asparagus
    & tofu
Sweet potato salad
Tomato soup

Rachael Anne Hill
Chicken & barley
    supper
Mackerel & bulghur
    wheat salad
Moroccan honey
    & lemon chicken
Mustardy mushroom
    stroganoff
Prawn & butter bean
    rice
Saffron fish pilaf
Spiced berry compote
White chocolate
    & raspberry fool

**Elsa Petersen-
Schepelern**
Baked stuffed
    pumpkin
Italian tuna & beans
Spicy butternut
    & chicken curry

Louise Pickford
Gingered chicken
    noodles
Pasta with melted
    ricotta
Thai-style beef salad

Jennie Shapter
Artichoke & ham
    tortilla
Chickpea tortilla
Feta cheese & tomato
    open omelette
Paella tortilla
Porcini frittata
Sun-dried tomato
    frittata

Sonia Stevenson
Braised lamb with okra
Brisket & vegetables
Brunswick stew
Caribbean vegetable
    stew
Fish mollee
Pork & bean casserole
Roast cod cutlets
Spicy chickpeas
Vietnamese-style beef

Linda Tubby
Baked rice with garlic
Baked sardines
Imam bayildi
Tuna & potato stew

Sunil Vijayakar
Beef madras
Red kidney bean curry

Fran Warde
Beef & carrot
    casserole
Bouillabaisse
Chicken & bacon pot
Chilli con carne
Easy fish stew
Lamb navarin
Lamb pilaf
Lancashire hotpot
Tuna fish cakes

Laura Washburn
Baked apples & pears
Chicken, sausage
    & rice
Creamy potato gratin
Greek-style omelette
Lamb stew with piri
    piri
Peach cobbler
Pepper & chorizo
    tortilla
Prawns with couscous
Spring lamb stew

photography credits

Caroline Arber
Pages 26, 117, 183,
200, 203, 204

Henry Bourne
Pages 15, 210

Martin Brigdale
Pages 6ac, 55, 62, 88r,
90, 93, 94, 95, 97, 103,
105, 110, 112, 118l,
118r, 120, 121, 123,
124, 128, 129, 142,
150, 151, 152, 156,
166c, 167, 168, 176,
191, 193

Peter Cassidy
Pages 6c, 6cr, 7, 16,
29, 36, 38, 43, 50, 57,
66, 85, 107, 108, 137,
146r, 147, 154, 155,
162, 164, 165, 170,
196, 218, 219, 220,
221, 222, 223, 225,
227

Nicki Dowey
Pages 88l, 113, 166r,
187

Tara Fisher
Pages 6ar, 46 all, 56,
59, 60, 63, 64, 67, 115

Caroline Hughes
Page 125

Richard Jung
Pages 2-3, 6al, 6cl, 6bl,
6bc, 8l, 8c, 9, 14, 25,
41, 68 all, 69, 70, 71,
73, 74, 77, 78, 81, 83,
88c, 89, 98, 102, 106,
109, 119, 139, 140,
146c, 159, 160, 166l,
174, 175, 180, 186,
212, 216r, 217, 230,
231

William Lingwood
Pages 4-5, 45, 143,
146l, 148, 179, 181,
195, 199, 207, 208,
211, 215

Diana Miller
Pages 27, 37, 76

David Munns
Pages 6br, 47, 51, 52,
101, 172, 188, 216l,
233, 234

Noel Murphy
Pages 22, 48, 114

William Reveall
Pages 8r, 30, 32, 33,
42, 82, 86, 87, 127,
131, 132, 133, 158,
184, 216c, 226, 229

Craig Robertson
Page 197

Yuki Sugiura
Pages 1, 10, 13, 17,
18

Debi Treloar
Pages 21, 144, 163,
171, 192

Pia Tryde
Pages 28, 92

Ian Wallace
Page 34

Kate Whitaker
Pages 118c, 135, 136

Francesca Yorke
Page 235